SACRED SCIENCE
of NUMBERS

A Series of Lecture Lessons Dealing with
the Sacred Science of Numbers

by Corinne Heline

 DEVORSS *Publications*

Seventh Printing 1991
ISBN: 0-87516-442-0

DeVorss & Company, Publisher
P.O. Box 550
Marina del Rey, CA 90294

Printed in the United States of America

TABLE OF CONTENTS

THE NUMBER ONE

"All is One issued from None."

God said, "Let there be Light, and there was
Light."   – *Genesis 1:3.*

An appropriate thought in connection with the reverential
approach to the study of numbers in relation to the Bible is
voiced in the following words of wisdom by Eusebius:
"Mathematical forms are but veils concealing from the vulgar
gaze divine things." The number 1 is represented in both Roman
and Arabic systems by a single upright line (1) but in the
various ancient systems where numerals were also used as letters,
the custom of substituting the letter A for the monad was
almost universal. Pythagoras, who has been immortalized by his
discoveries and teachings in relation to the Divine Science of
Numbers, stated: The Monad is the beginning of all things.

One is masculine.

One is Fire.

One is the unity from which all manifestation proceeds.

One is the primordial Ray which issued forth at the
command of God:

"Let there be Light."

One is the great White Flame which holds all the seven
colors in latency or suspension.

One is the great primordial Fiat in power, rhythm,
motion, and color, that set into operation the forces that
are made manifest in the Seven Days of Creation as
described biblically in the first chapter of Genesis.

We must come into the realization at the very outset of our

study that there is a vast difference between numbers and figures. Numbers are representative of forces which operate on the highest spiritual planes. Figures are but the external hieroglyphs of these spiritual powers as they may be seen and studied upon this outer physical plane. Numbers are the ten supreme Principles upon which the universe (not alone our solar system) is founded. Figures are but the outer shadow-forms of these all-abiding Principles as they are comprehended and interpreted by man.

The Bible, that high climax in spiritual lore, is founded upon this basic spiritual functioning of Numbers. And it is in an endeavor to present something of this profound and deeply concealed truth in relation to the power and significance of Numbers that this series of lesson-lectures has been prepared.

All phases of occult instruction are to be found in our Christian Bible. As we turn our attention to its numerical teaching, new and far-reaching vistas open before us, and wondrous indeed are the mighty truths which this phase of its interpretation contains.

Every number possesses an individual keynote, and every book in the Bible is "set" or attuned to one of these fundamental numbers. As we gain some comprehension of the spiritual meaning of these several keynotes, we shall discover also new and deeper meanings in the various Bible books with which they are in attunement.

All creation proceeds from unity, and all manifested things must return and be resolved again into unity. Herein is to be found the involutionary and evolutionary cycles of progression, both spiritual and material.

As all forces of outer expression upon this earth planet were once a component part of the sun, they will eventually return to their source and be resolved back into unity. This is action in harmony with cyclic law. Both involution and evolution are forces of unity in diversity. They are projections of the Supreme

Center, emanations of the One for purposes of growth, development, expansion, and experience. From this we may understand that 1 signifies the highest phase of self-expression possible to human comprehension. The early Christians, who as esotericists were students of the spiritual significance of numbers, described the Monad or the One as unity with the godhead.

We shall approach the study of spiritual numerology both from the cosmic and the personal viewpoints.

One represents the Light of the Old Testament Dispensation. It also represents light in the New Testament Dispensation, but it is now the man in whom the Christ Light is born within. This follows from the fact that 1 is Fire − the Fire of God, and the manifestation of this divine principle in man.

Numerically interpreted, 1 is the foundation tone and dominant note of the musical scale. It has two methods of progress only, namely, the giving forth of itself and the return to its original source or center. By reason of this sacrifice of itself in selfless giving, it always returns to a higher central focus as, for instance, in the ever-ascending series of the octave in the musical scale.

The Ancient Wisdom declares: "From One Light, Seven Lights; from each of the Seven, Seven times Seven." And again: "The One Spark descends from the Great Flame. It journeys through the seven worlds. In the first it is a stone. It passes into the second, and behold − a plant. In the third it becomes an animal. In the fourth, the Thinker is born." Such is the strength and majesty of One.

The monad, as previously stated, is a Fire number, and its flame is white. God, who is the source of all the great world religions, has always been worshipped as an all-consuming Fire or Emanation from the Great Unknowable.

Unity is the supreme First Cause, the reason and purpose of all creation. All things are inherently divine because they are emanations of this supernal Unity. These creations of the One must be perfected before they are again drawn into their single central source. Thus we discover that the purpose of evolution is but to further the forces of unity and to bring into being a greater manifestation of the One, both in the universe and in man. In other words, the processes of both involution and evolution are embraced within the operations of the One, and have for their purpose the spiritualization both of the earth and of man. They constitute, in other words, the redemptive processes of matter.

Numbers represent initial fundamental principles of harmony or Godhood. The sooner we come to understand something of the operation of these basic principles, and learn to regulate our being in conformity with them, the sooner we shall be lifted into the freedom of a new light that knows no longer the shackles of poverty, disease, and death. It is a knowledge that will enable us to realize ourselves, in the words of Paul, as "heirs and joint heirs with Christ."

The Law of Vibration is a reaction of the expression of Unity in manifestation. A study of this law is becoming increasingly important for the spiritually awakened scientist. The secrets of transforming the mind and regenerating the body are to be found therein.

When an ego finds its own number, it has found the path of its own highest self-expression. It has learned the way to connect with the innate divinity, the primal source of its own inner guidance or light, the power of the awakened Christ within.

The 1 in its personal relationship, is the ego, or the divine spirit represented by the single column or shaft of life, and which bears the glorious heritage of a self-conscious divinity. Infinite are the depths of wisdom concealed within this spirit. This wisdom will be revealed in all its luminosity and power when a bridge has been built in consciousness connecting the outer understanding with the inner hidden soul wisdom. It is to this inner soul wisdom which extends beyond the ages, that veiled ISIS had reference when she declared: "I am all that ever has been, all that is, and all that ever shall be, and no mortal shall ever lift my veil". Even to the greatest human knowledge this inner wisdom is a "light that shineth in the darkness, but which the "dark comprehendeth not".

It is the promise of the New Age that we shall see no more through a glass darkly, but face to face. By the operations of the One we shall be able to enter into a conscious realization, here and now, of our immortality. We shall no longer live in the erroneous belief that heaven is to be reached only through death, but in the living knowledge that we have but to go into the depths of our own consciousness and there claim the divine values of our eternal selfhood. As a pillar of fire rising triumphantly upward to the stars, the 1 proclaims the glorious truth. Its emblem is, very fittingly, a crown. Among the books of the Bible, Ezekiel, with its sublime heaven-world imagery, is an expression of the majesty of 1.

We study the monad from the viewpoints of both the absolute and the relative. From the viewpoint of the absolute, 1 has been aptly described as the "heavenly celibate working in Chaos". It finds biblical expression in the fiat: "Let there be Light!" From the viewpoint of the relative, the celestial monad, the inherent god-man, which is a spark from the Celestial Plane, is set forth upon its evolutionary journey under the guidance of innumerable hosts, returning to its original source only after having fanned the spark into a flame.

In its first projection, the monad or 1 expresses its inherent dynamic quality as a vertical line of gleaming blue light, an upright pillar of scintillating, dazzling brilliancy. Aided by other Celestial Hosts, the evolving monad later awakens within itself more of its potential godhood, giving it expression in a glory of golden light. A further step toward earth embodiment brings to the monad the first lessons in form building. It now takes on its initial robe of red flame, which marks its first contact with the third of the primary colors, red.

Individualization, self-expression, epigenesis, and initiative — these are the keywords belonging to 1. In the long evolutionary development undertaken by man for the purpose of unfolding the divine latencies into manifested actualities, two distinct paths open before him. Whichever he chooses, he will give expression to the principle of 1 but in the one instance it will be in its lower aspects, in the other, in its higher. On the lower plane the 1 will function as aggressive self-will, egotism, and braggadosio. The powers of the 1 have not yet transcended the limited personal life. On the higher plane the 1 will express itself through the impersonal self or spirit in terms of spiritual endeavor and universal objectives. This state was exemplified by the Immortal Twelve whose lives were completely dedicated to loving, selfless service. With them the personal had been lifted up to the impersonal so that they were able to enter into the transcendent experience of being moved by the pentecostal tongues of flame.

Moses, when looking upon the Burning Bush that was not consumed by the flaming fire, contacted the fire of the immortal one within himself. Elijah experienced a yet further development of this same sacred fire of the One when his consciousness was raised to a level enabling him to transcend the experience of death. The experience of the three holy men in the fiery furnace is another instance of like significance. When we learn to abide within the light of this inner flame, we are immune to all external dangers and hurts. We then walk in the light as He is in the light. Only then shall we know the highest meanings of the number One.

There is an ancient Rosicrucian admonition which says: "procure a six-penny lamp, keep it supplied with oil and you will be able to light at its flame all the lamps and candles and fires of the whole world without diminishing its flame". Meditation on the deep truth concealed in that statement will bring light on the significance of the number 1.

Neither in its essential reality nor in its highest expression can the number 1 ever manifest anything but perfect harmony. Any apparent diversity is but an illusion of the senses in relation to the external world. Those attuned to 1 should of all people have the least difficulty in learning how to contact the divine center within, and to organize the inner and the outer life in accordance with the Law which is perfect and unalterable.

The 1 never knows defeat. Those who come under its law have learned that "the only failure is in ceasing to try". They are always conscious within themselves of the admonition: "Be ye perfect even as your Father in heaven is perfect". Nothing short of this high ideal can ultimately and permanently satisfy the 1.

Evolution begins with 1. In it inheres Divinity. Evolution also closes with 1 at the completion of the long cycle when all things are again at perfect at-one-ment with the Divine. This is the significance of the circled serpent holding its own tail in its mouth. This is at once a symbol of the 1 and the crown of immortal life.

That estatic soul vision known biblically as the book of Ezekiel, which when interpreted in relation to its inner meanings, is concerned not only with the times and conditions in which it was written, but is also a revelation of the glories of the new day and the new age that man is soon to know. It reveals the majesty of the dispensation of Air wherein increasing and mighty wonder-workings of God shall be unfolded. As previously mentioned, these visions of Ezekiel, the prophetic seer, are attuned to the numerical emanations of 1.

The twelve tribes of Israel represent in the light of the New Age understanding, certain qualifications and principles that are correlated with the twelve zodiacal signs. These principles must be evolved within all men as necessary requisites for becoming a part of the new race which will usher in the Dispensation of Air, which we more frequently refer to as the coming Aquarian Age. To each of these specified tribes, Ezekiel has given a certain "portion" or rather the "portion of One".

We can understand more comprehensively the meaning of this statement as we realize that 1 in its highest relationships, means a return to the original source, a reunion with the divinity within. One stands for the attainment of the "single eye", that is, single to that only which is good and true, and which manifests the powers of the Christ man within, knowing only the innate divinity in all creation. This is the rightful heritage of 1 and whoever learns to manifest it will also come to know the glories of that same holy city which was revealed in the vision beheld by the enraptured Ezekiel. In spiritual symbology, "city" means a state of consciousness. It is the city whose gates (centers of spiritual ingress) bore the names of the twelve tribes, each bearing the signature or power of 1. (Ezekiel: 48:30). The ablations offered by the priests (the holy or illumined ones) within the sanctuary (the sacred or inner place) numbered 10. This signifies unity in its highest expression wherein oneness is realized with all good. Such a realization belongs to the New Age and for those coming under the law of 1, is the prime essential for the development of their highest faculties and the accomplishment of their supreme destiny.

"The Past, the Present, the Future —
The everlasting Trinity in One.
The Great Illusion of the Absolute."

— — — —

KEY THOUGHTS
"Unity contains all Force and is the cause of all things."

In the Ten Principles or Numbers is outlined the "dip of spirit into matter, the experiences engendered thereby, and the final restoration in spirit.

> Finite and infinite are two principles of
> world-creation. Numbers are divine and things
> in themselves. One and the whole clearly belong
> to the sphere of the infinite. Whereas the parts
> and plurality belong to the sphere of the finite.
> — Pappus translation of Euclid's
> Book X on *The Elements.*

As in the consideration of the monad, we shall observe the duad first from the universal or cosmic viewpoint and afterward from the personal angle.

In a study of the duad we find the beginnings of division, separation, duality, contrasts. Pythagoras says: "Two is the imperfect condition into which being falls when it becomes detached from the Monad of God. Spiritual beings emanating from God are enveloped in the Duad and therefore receive only illusory impressions."

The symbol or numeral of the figure 2 represents the descent of spirit into matter. God moves on he face of the waters to create. So the masculine principle of God operates in conjunction with the powers of the erstwhile prostrate feminine principle and thus it is that all formative processes begin. In this manner the firmament was made manifest. The waters which were under the firmament were divided from the waters which were above the firmament; and there was evening and there was morning a second day. (Genesis 1:7-8) The duad is the silent secretive, mysterious, occult feminine principle — the power behind the throne, as it were, unheralded and unseen, yet innermost heart and life of all created essences.

The fundamental of Pythagorean mathematics is given as follows: "The first natural division of numbers is into even and odd. An even number is one which is divisible into two equal parts without leaving a monad between them. All even numbers (except the duad) may be divided into two equal parts, and also into two unequal parts. For example, 8 divides into 4 and 4, and also into 5 and 3; 6 into 3 and 3, and also into 4 and 2; 4 into 2 and 2, and also into 3 and 1; 10 into 5 and 5, as well as into 7 and 3." The duad, being composed only of two simple unities, allows no such further division. The reason for this will be considered in the delineation of the number 11.

The ten great principles or numbers are focussing points or attractive mediums of high cosmic forces, and without these central transmitting stations there could be no manifest or visible creation.

In the second phase of God-manifestation, known as the initial home of the great Feminine by reason of the necessary evolutionary processes of differentiation, the first veils of illusion are manifest. The duad is the first center in which is experienced sorrow and sacrifice. It is out of its pain and grief and sacrificial service that the Spirit of Beauty is first born.

Let us understand that when dealing with the high realms of the first beginnings of God-manifestation, we are dealing with purely abstract ideas. The Kaballah defines beauty as follows: "Beauty is the luminous conception of equilibrium in form; it is the mediating principle between Creator and the created."

The nearer we approach the inner and deeper comprehension of the duad, the more intimate will become our appreciation and realization of beauty. We have associated beauty with mere externalities for so long that we find it difficult to grasp its significance in terms of an inner revealing and transforming power. It is only as we reawaken the sleeping, or fallen, feminine factor with, — that factor which is the great formative principle of the duad or Word potency of God — that we shall discover anew the latent powers of beauty and come to understand how and why its attributes are always so closely associated with the feminine pole of man's being. "Beauty is Truth, Truth is Beauty. That is all ye know and all ye need to know." The poet sang these high words from an exalted place of inner knowing.

The monad and the duad, the masculine and the feminine, form the two columes upon which all world structures are founded. They are the Strength and the Beauty of the mystic seer of biblical times, King Solomon, whose name in three languages means 'the wisdom of the Sun'. It was in the light of the dual process of form-building that Solomon composed these strange, sphinx-like utterances which we know as the Book of Ecclesiastes.

The far-reaching symbolism of the Masonic Lodge is builded around the mystery of the sleeping Feminine. It is only as this hidden truth is comprehended by a Lodge that it awakens to its ability and opportunity to serve as a center of manifested working power for the betterment of man. Its possibilities as such a unit of service are as yet undreamed of by the great majority of this noble Fraternity. Jah-Hovah in Hebrew is the Male-Female life operating in the highest realms of spirit, and which is reflected in the lower worlds as sex. The name Jehovah, in its final analysis, signifies the Law of Polarity by which alone man is made complete.

The color of 2 is gold. It is the golden Water of Life that brings form out of Chaos. Evil and misfortune have long been associated with duality and hence with the number 2; The Romans dedicated the second month to Pluto, God of the underworld, and on the second day of this particular month it was their custom to offer sacrifices to the Manos, or the spirits of the dead. This association of evil with the duad comes from the introduction of duality into human consciousness on the lower or illusive planes. In the higher realms, as we have previously seen, duality is polarity, or the alternating cycles of rhythm and harmony which is all good. On the lower or deceptive rounds we lose sight of this high truth, and in this loss know only the alternation of extremes, namely, light and dark, heat and cold, life and death, youth and age, disease and health, poverty and wealth, sorrow and joy, war and peace, friends and enemies.

The ego vacillating between the varied experiences of those two opposites has learned to associate misfortune with 2 because, as previously noted, it is in the heart of the duad that sorrow is born through this process of diversity or alternation. An illustration of this fact may be observed in the history of English kings. Those who have borne the II of any name have been the bearers of sorrow and misfortune. William II, Edward II, and Richard II were all murdered.

The Ten Principles are magnetic centers of force and represent, not arbitrary, but potential and universal powers. The spiritual tendency of numbers is to raise all that come under their influence above their present limitations. Remembering in this connection that Beauty and Truth characterize the inmost being of the duad, it is to these qualities that consciousness must rise in order to avoid the misfortune and the sorrow so commonly associated with 2. The two person must learn to tune into that high plane of being wherein there is no shadow of turning. He must learn to focus his consciousness in life rather than in death, in light rather than in darkness.

Joshua, the best beloved disciple of Moses, and the greatest of the Old Dispensation teachers, and John, the beloved of our Lord, the Christ, and the supreme Evangel of the New Day, are illustrious examples of individuals who have demonstrated the ability to rise above the limitations of the human vibratory rate of 2 and raise it to its initial celestial degree in which it sounds the "word that was with God and the Word that was God and without which not anything was made that was made."

Proclus wrote: "The Duad is the medium between Unity and Number, for unity by addition produces more than by multiplication; the duad whether added to itself or multiplied by itself produces the same."

The duad symbolizes both love and sacrifice because it was willing to separate itself from the central source, or the monad, and to undergo the sorrowful experiences which this separation entailed in order that it might thereby further the evolution of life.

In the creation story of Genesis we have the following account of how the one became two:

> And the Lord God caused a deep sleep to fall upon Adam and he slept, and He took one of his ribs and closed up the flesh instead thereof: and the rib which the Lord God had taken from man, made he a woman and brought her unto the man. And Adam said, 'this is now bone of my bones and flesh of my flesh; she shall be called woman because she was taken out of man'.
>
> *— Genesis 2:21-23*

The sorrow of 2 grows out of the deep and ever-recurrent spirit-recollection which it has of this separation, and also out of its loneliness and longing for a return to unity. The early Christian esotericists identified the highest expression of 2 with the power of the Holy Ghost, or union with Christ.

With the Fall of man came the subjection of spirit to matter. The monad lost its glorious light and became submerged by the seductive, illusory projections of the duad.

> And the eyes of them both were opened and they knew that they were naked. And they heard the voice of the Lord God walking in the garden in the cool of the day, and Adam and his wife hid themselves from the presence of the Lord God amongst the trees of the garden.   *— Genesis 3:7-8*

Since that introduction of dualtiy into the consciousness ages ago, man has been conscious of two selves, the higher and the lower, or as the German scientists describe it, the "me and the not-me". So long as man is conscious only of the not-me, or personality, the mere outer reflection of the duad, he will remain subject to the cycles of alternation, and suffer the impacts of their extremities, experiencing to the full the sorrows of this illusory existence. The more severe these impacts, the sooner will the real man awaken from his delusive dream and learn to discriminate between the real and the unreal, the flase and the true. It is thus that he will learn in time to distinguish clearly between the me and the not-me, which is the great aim and purpose of the repetition of the life cycles upon the earth planet.

All the important characters in biblical history have the dual consciousness represented in their lives in the symbology of women. In some instances the woman represents the lower aspect of the feminine principle, in others, the higher. Each of the illustrious Bible characters has at some time or other stood at the cross-roads of decision, and not until the union with the higher was accomplished, was there the light and the power necessary for the performance of those great works which made them immortal.

To illustrate: In the legend of Abraham, we find both Hagar and Sarah; in the experiences of Jacob, we observe the dominance of Leah and Rachel; in the life of Lazarus, Martha and Mary; and in that of Christ Jesus, the supreme Way-Shower for all men, we note the influence of Mary Magdalene and the blessed Virgin Mary, the Madonna.

When man awakens to an awareness of the "me", the true spirit-man within, he begins the ascent of the mountain peaks of consciousness such as Abraham knew in his communion with the angels; and that Jacob found in his ecstatic vision; and which Lazarus experienced in the glories of his resurrection day; and which the Christ attained to on the mountain peaks of the Transfiguration and the Ascension.

In such illumined contacts the true spirit power of the 2 is born; the path of regeneration and redemption is found.

In connection with this lesson, the student is requested to study the seventh chapter of Romans and to meditate long and carefully upon the truths contained therein. In it Paul has outlined the operation of this dual consciousness in man and the results that attend each phase of its development.

> For I was alive without the law once, but when the commandment came, sin revived and I died. And the commandment which was ordained to life, I found to be unto death.   — *Romans 7:9-10*

The two upright columns of the Masonic Lodge, the Jachin and Boaz, represent the highest manifestation of the duad. The elaborate ceremonial of the Lodge is designed for the lofty purpose of assisting the participants to regenerate their natures and raise the fallen feminine principle to its proper place. In the symbolism of the Lodge, the broken pillar must be restored; equilibrium must be reestablished. Not until this is done can that glorious temple, "not made with hands, but eternal in the heavens" be erected.

The Theosophical arithmetic states: "One is the spirit of the living God. It is the name of Him who liveth forever. Two is the spirit from this spirit. In it He engraved the 22 letters."

Two is the formative mother principle, the heart. It is the Keeper of the Cosmic Records. Two is the emotional life, unleashed on the lower planes, and transmuted on the higher.

The words 'seer' and 'gold' both vibrate to 2. In the Book of Joshua in the Old Testament and in the Gospel of John in the New, we are given instructions as to how to subjugate the emotions, how to lift them up, and how to make the heart the great love center of the body. When the work outlined in these instructions has been accomplished, true seership is attained, and the soul is robed in a luminous wedding garment fashioned of the purest gold of the spirit. Such was the attainment of John the Divine, and, also in a lesser degree, of Joshua, whose privilege it was to lead the Israelites into the Promised Land. Those coming under the vibratory law of 2 are admonished to study frequently the books by both John and Joshua.

The number 1 is symbolized by the crown; the number 2 is symbolized by the cross. The crown and the cross are inseparably associated because they are essentially one, being different and separate in a relative sense only. One is identified with the head and the crown; Two relates to the heart and the cross. When the mystic marriage of the head and the heart is consummated, the cross becomes the yoke that is easy and the burden that is Light − the Light of the crown of Immortal Life.

Two on the material plane manifests as *duality*, and in its lower aspect expresses itself as indecision, purposelessness, and vacillation. On the higher or spiritual plane, Two manifests as equilibrium, which may be characterized as balance, poise and steadfastness. These higher qualifications may be noted as representative of the life and attainments of both Joshua and John, the beloved disciple. They both typify the highest attributes of 2.

The keynote of the Book of Joshua may be summed up in the single word 'Jehovah' with the full singification of all its meanings. Jehovah is a four-power word. Four is an accentuation and doubling of the life forces of 2. In his final admonition to his disciples, Joshua differentiates between the evil and the good, or the high and the low manifestations of 2. It is to the manifestation of the lower aspects of 2 that Hoshua refers in the words: "Choose you this day whom ye shall serve, whether the gods which your fathers served that were beyond the River, or the gods of the Amorites in whose land ye dwell; but as for me and my house, we will serve Jehovah." — *Joshua 24:15*

The name John digits twenty (20), which is 2 complemented by the cipher. This implies tremendously increased working power of 2. The naught symbolizes the mysteries of infinitude which we can appropriate in terms of sublimation and the consciousness of the Absolute. It is the power that lifts above and beyond the limited spheres of life and death as we know these alternating phases of being on this mundane plane. It represents that unbroken and untrampled existence into which the spirit of John had ascended, and to which the supreme Lord of Life and Death referred when He said; "If I will that he tarry till I come, what is that to thee?" (John 21:23). May the Two inspired by this illustrious example lift unto this same exalted consciousness and state of being.

QUESTIONS FOR NUMBER TWO

1. What role in the redemptive process of matter do you consider is represented by 2?
2. What connection do you find between 2 and the second zodiacal sign, Taurus?
3. Name a biblical character who you consider correlated to the forces of 2?
4. Give some keywords particularly descriptive of 2.

NOTE: These lessons are not intended for casual reading, but for careful study and meditation wherein it is hoped that by a lifting of consciousness the student may be able to contact the inner man, — that source of light eternal which makes life complete both within and without.

THE NUMBER THREE

> Three is a triple Word, for the Hierarchical
> Order always Manifests itself by Three. The
> Word simple, the Word hieroglyphic, the Word
> symbolic; or the Word that expresses, the Word
> that conceals, the Word that signifies. All
> hieratic intelligence is in the perfect knowledge
> of these three degrees.   – *Pythagoras*

The inner illumination revealed by the ancient Greek philosopher in the above passage was also shared by John, a later disciple of the Mysteries, as is indicated in the opening lines of his Gospel: "The word was God, the word was with God, and without it was not anything made that was made."

The above passages of both John and Pythagoras are the fruits of meditation on cosmic truths. They give evidence of an understanding of something of the formation of the Formative Triad or threefold power of the Godhead. The early sages defined the outpourings of this Triplicity as the World of Emanation, the World of Creation, and the World of Formation. John describes this same process as the word that was God, the word that was with God and the word that became flesh and dwelt among men.

The force and power of 3 has been identified with the Trinity by the Wise Men throughout the ages. All great world religions worship a three-fold Godhead. It is one of religion's fundamental teachings. In our Christian terminology the three persons of the Godhead are the Father, the Son and the Holy Ghost.

One projects from itself 2; from the component parts of 1 and 2, 3 is formed. The spirit of God (1) moves on the face of the waters (2) in order to create (3). In accordance with this mathematical principle, all created things have come into manifestation. In relation to this truth Pythagoras says: "Every Triad is hung to a Monad."

As we meditate upon these processes in manifestation throughout all creation, we comprehend anew something of the profound significance of that Masonic admonition: "Brother, study nature for it bears the stamp of Divinity."

Paracelsus writes regarding the mighty power of 3: "Remember, therefore, there are of Things Primordial but three. From these take two, and from these again, if thou judge rightly, one more. The Triple Thing will then consist of Gold alone".

John observes this same process when he writes: "Whosoever denieth the Son, the same hath not the Father, but he that acknowledgeth the Son hath the Father also. If ye continue in the Son and in the Father, this is the promise that He hath promised us, even eternal life". – John 2:23-25.

In the outer world of manifestation the unity is ever becoming the Trinity, or Trinity is ever detaching itself and returning again into the One. Thus do we note the ceaseless activity of nature about us and the transitoriness of all form.

One is the supreme primal cause, 2 is that cause in manifestation, and 3 is the product or result of the combined operations of 1 and 2. In order to comprehend the significance of 3 we must know the creative powers of 1 and 2.

Again the high inspiration of John declares: "For there are three that bear record in heaven, the Father, the Son, and the Holy Ghost; and these three are one. And there are three that bear witness in earth, the spirit and the water and the blood, and these three agree in one". John 5:7,8.

The equilateral triangle is a symbol of perfection, for it contains the father and mother principles, or the 1 and the 2 in harmonious proportion. The true and eternal purpose of evolution is to perfect this equilibrium or polarity in man. The supreme object of nature, therefore, is the proper blending of the qualities of 1 and 2 to the end that it may produce as a result the Christed individual. In Masonic ceremonialism this fact is represented by the Sun, Moon and Mercury, or the Master of the Lodge. Note, also, that the Masonic Wisdom has placed the letter G in the center of the equilateral triangle. In some symbologies the Hebrew letter Yod, the tenth letter of the alphabet, is used instead of the letter G. In each instance, the letter is representative of the innate creative power through which all things are produced upon all planes of manifestation.

Three is the number of degrees or steps in all schools of inner illumination. In the esoteric school of the early Christians these were referred to as steps of Purification, Illumination, and Bringing to Light. They constituted a part of the Rite of the Love Feast, or Agape, described in the Acts of the Apostles. In the Masonic Fraternity the three degrees are familiar to us as those of the Apprentice the Fellowcraft, and the Master. They represent the modern survival of a fragment of the magnificent symbolism of the Ancient Wisdom as this was known and practiced by the Hierophants of earlier days. In the life of the supreme Teacher those three degrees or steps are represented by the Baptism, the Transfiguration, and the Resurrection. Pythagoras gave utterance to a deep mystic truth when he said: "All Hieratic intelligence is in the perfect knowledge of these three degrees".

The three primary colors, blue yellow, and red, are radiations of the three-fold Godhead, and produce upon earth the varying manifestations of life, consciousness, and form. A realization of this fact, together with a fuller understanding of man's own relation to the powers of the Trinity, will in time, bring forth an entirely new system of healing and a new technique of human regeneration. The new methods for helping man to recover wholeness and uprightness will be based upon the forces of color as these relate to man's expanding consciousness.

"Rule your work through one thing", says Paracelsus. "Proceeding from Unity to Duality, and thence to Three things; then travel to Cyprus. There you will be refused nothing. Afterward for these Three build a tabernacle, and diligently take heed that the sacred Threefoldness be reduced through Duality to Unity — the Author of all consummate perfection."

In those few sentences this great seer has described the way out from God, through evolution, into external plane existence, and the path of return, through regeneration, to a final union with God-consciousness. In the light of this conception, we begin to understand the important and frequent use of the number 3 throughout the Bible, since in this Textbook of Life this same story is presented in many variations and by numerous incidents. "Magic", declares Paracelsus further, "has three books. Firstly, theology; secondly, medicine; thirdly, astronomy. Whence the Magus knows and worships Trinity in Unity and imparts the power he receives from God to suffering mortals". — "By their fruits ye shall know them".

The third day of creation produced the *tree whose seed is within itself*, and which yields fruit after its own kind. For those who come under the numerical law of 3, meditation upon the truth contained in these words will be of invaluable assistance toward gaining a realization of the powers within which are awaiting unfoldment. To 3 belong honor, fame, and beauty. The word 'adept', like one who has attained the status it signifies, represents the evolved powers of 3. The symbol of the number is a wreath, which in turn represents eternity or the ever-abiding power of its high aspect of Truth.

Some predominant figures of the Bible who express the high characteristics of 3 are the prophets Isaiah and Hosea, and the disciple Matthew, the writer of the first Gospel.

One of the greatest of our modern mystics, Franz Hartman,

says: "Try to find out the spiritual significance of the Triangle, and learn to know thyself".

Since we are living in a world of three dimensional consciousness, the law of 3 operates with us universally. All religions are founded upon tenets embracing the evolution of spirit, soul, and body. Wherever we find the number 3 in parable, or used in the life history of the various biblical characters, the key to its deeper meaning may be found through tracing their relation to the threefold nature of man, namely, the spirit, soul, and body.

Each letter and number bears its own secret story in color, tone, and vibratory rhythm or power. Digit the letters of a name, and something of its inner significance begins to unfold. The digit of vowels marks the spiritual path and the digit of consonants, the material urge. When 1, 2, and 3 are in harmonious relationship in a name, they indicate that its bearer has a splendid working trinity with which to gain a rich and plenteous harvest from many and varied experiences upon this outer physical plane. The higher spiritual trinity we shall study at length when we come to a consideration of the number 11, and the universal or cosmic consciousness which this higher trinity reveals, presaging as it does, the further evolution of the spirit, soul, and body of man.

> He gave to each one a number and a name which
> only he knew who received it.   — *Revelations 11:17*

Three is expansive, unlimited, a "free" number, as evidenced in the utterances of the inspired Isaiah, who, scorning subterfuge, convention, and old established customs, renounced prestige, position, and, finally, life itslef, in order that he might teach truth as he received it. The same urge of the number 3 operated in the life of Matthew, the great emancipator, whose life and works may well be described in the following words of

Paracelsus: "A resurrection from the dead in which soul, body and spirit after purification came together again, – a new spiritual man".

The color of 3 is Golden Flame or Illumined Gold. It represents the dross of the lower nature lifted up and transmuted into the radiance of a new life, its aura being as white as snow, and as golden as the Sun.

The predominant urge of 3, despite its manifold opportunities for material experiences, is an all-permeating desire for a return to a union with 1, the indwelling Diety which is a reflection in man of that "One apart and transcending the Three"

Hear, O Israel, the Lord our God is One Lord.– *Deut. 6:4*

I am the Lord and there is no God beside me: I girded thee though thou hast not known me. – *Isaiah 45:5*

And the scribe said unto him: "Well Master thou hast said the truth, for there is one God and there is none other but He." – *Mark 12:32*

In that unfathomed Sphinx Book of the Bible, Ecclesiastes, chapter IV verses 8 to 12, Solomon, the wise numerologist, has given the perfect law underlying the cosmic Trinity of One, Two, and Three.

"When One willed to create, One became many (each threefold). The First were the most blessed and mighty Three, to be His ministers". Herein are stated the fundamentals upon which the doctrine of the Trinity is based.

The Ancient Wisdom declares: "Besides triplicity which exists in elements and all created subjects, there is another more mystical and obscure triplicity which is recognized by Adepts. Without this latter, true spiritual power cannot be obtained. These three principles key to all nature. The first in One is a pure white virgin. The Bride of God and the stars through which as a medium, all things were and are made in nature and in art".

These words describe the golden flame which is the soul color of 3, and point the way of the transmutation process whereby this high soul radiance may be attained. "I was once dead, but now I live". The principle of life which animates the physical body may become the luminous radiance of the soul body. "He that ascends is the same as he that descends".

Thus we see that life and death are interrelated principles. As St. Martin observes: "If the number 3 is imposed upon all things, it is because it presided at their origin. Had there been four instead of three elements, they would have been indestructible and the world eternal; being three, they are devoid of permanent existence because they are without unity, as will be clear to those who know the true law of numbers. There can be Three in One in the Divine Triad, but not One in Three, because that which is One in Three is subject to death".

The keynote of 3 is activity, on the lower physical planes, and in the mass mind of man this activity principle operates as disintegration. In the higher realms and in the consciousness of the Illumined, it operates as transmutation.

We find the operation of this threefold power instanced n the lives of Adam and Noah, and represented in both cases by their three sons.

The working Trinity as symbolized by the three sons of Adam:

    1. Cain — The Fire or Creative principle of One.

    2. Abel — The Water or Sustaining principle of Two.

    3. Seth — The transmuting activity principle of Three.

The working Trinity, as symbolized by the three sons of Noah:

    1. Shem —˙ The Fire or Creative principle of One.

    2. Japeth — The Water or Sustaining principle of Two.

    3. Ham — The Activity or disintegrating principle of

Three.

We note in the workings of this threefold power in man that the three sons both of Adam and of Noah typify not personalities, but principles. As we follow the experiences recounted in both legends, and note the destruction and chaos which result from the deeds of both Cain and Ham, we are observing the inharmonious effects of this threefold power in operation on the lower or material plane of being. The same results are to be noted in the life of the masses of humanity at the present time, since but few as yet have learned the operation in mind and spirit of the higher law connected with this threefold power. The wise know this law in its aspect of transmutation, whereas, the unwise are subject to its aspect of disintegration. The two processes are exemplified in the lives of Seth and Shem, and Cain and Ham respectively.

Just so long as the destructive force is paramount in the world, we shall have the despairing lament of Cain: "Every man's hand is against me". This will continue to sound the keynote of nations and of individuals until the forces of construction gain ascendancy.

Abel and Japeth represent the processes of awakening and enlightenment. The great forward step for humanity is described in the words of Eve, the intuitive consciousness, when at the birth of Seth, she exclaims in exultation: "God hath appointed me another seed instead of Abel". It is interesting to also note that "all the days of Seth were nine hundred and twelve years", which digits Three.

KEY THOUGHTS

The Chinese say numbers begin at One, are made perfect at Three, and terminate at Ten.

* * *

In the numbers from 1 to 10 we find outlined the path of generation and the way of regeneration.

Alchemy teaches that "the principle of the alchemists' magestery is 1, 4, 3, 2, and 1. — One is the unit from which all things come. Four are the elements of which all matter is composed. Three is Salt, Sulphur and Mercury. Two is Rebis, the volatile and fixed. One is the Stone, or that which is the fruit of the processes in all Hermetic labors."

Pythagoras called 4 the symbol of the Eternal Principle of Creation. Of a man who once came to him asking what he could teach him, Pythagoras inquired in turn, "Can you count?" The student replied by commencing to count: "1, 2, 3, 4." at which point Pythagoras interrupted him. "Stop there," said he, "Four is our sacred number."

Relative to this teaching of Pythagoras, we find the following diagram in the works of Franz Hartmann.

| Spirit | Soul | Fire | Air | Son | Father |
| Word | Man | Water | Earth | Christ Jesus | Holy Ghost |

Eternal Wisdom   Natural & Finite   Corner Stone

"He who truly knows Christ has well employed his time."

By mystic sages long antedating Pythagoras, 4 was considered the greatest of divine numbers, and was designated as the "quaternary." The holy name of Jehovah is expressed by the

Hebrew letters Yod-He-Vau-He, and it is also frequently designated by One, Two, Three, Four, these numbers having reference to the sacred Four. Four represents the Principle of Creation manifesting as the four elements out of which all things are created. This is the meaning of the four rivers which flowed out of the Garden of Eden and watered the face of the entire earth. The four elements, out of which all things are created, are recognized upon this physical plane as fire, air, water and earth. On the higher or invisible planes these elements are recognized as spiritual forces. When they work harmoniously and in unison, a powerful nucleus of both spiritual and material power is generated which manifests the rhythm of 4 on all planes of manifestation.

Four letters compose the Sacred Name of nearly all the gods who have been worshipped by the human race. Note the following: Isis — Egyptian; Assur and Nebo — Assyrian; Deus — Latin; Odin — Scandinavian; Dieu — French; Gott — German; Zues — Greek; Atma — Hindu; and Jove — Roman. In Egypt the God who created mortal, or dust man, bore the name of Ptah. And in Hebrew we have that most sacred and magical name, the Tetragrammaton.

The Gnostics declared that the Triangle, or 3, is God, and that 1 is man, whereas the 4 is God in man. To the man who is God-like we may therefore ascribe the awakened spiritual powers of 4. Four designates a transition of consciousness in ever-increasing and ascending rates of vibration. Four is the door of Illumination or Initiation. The Initiate transcends the planes of a three-dimensional knowledge and understanding, his faculties having expanded to such a degree that he is able to function in the realms of the fourth dimension. Solomon, the wise king of the Old Testament Dispensation, represents the highest development of Four.

In 4 we find the number carrying the power to create and to attain. When the forms of 4 are centered on the material plane they manifest as creative abilities; when focused in the spiritual, they give the ability to open new avenues for investigation in the psychic and spiritual realms.

Thus teaches the. Ancient Wisdom: "The Fourth Spoke of the great chain is our Mother Earth. Reach the 'Fourth Fruit' of the Fourth Path of Knowledge that leads to Nirvana, and thou shalt comprehend for thou shalt see."

Four is the sacred Tetrahtis, the "Mystic Square" of the Illumined of all peoples. Most interesting is the symbology of 4 in our Christian Bible. Four represents the powers of the Cherubim which manifest as scintillating flames. These celestial Beings guard the gates of Eden with their swords of flame; they stand as guardians before the portals of the Temple of King Solomon; and as John testifies in the recorded vision which he beheld on the Isle of Patmos, they surround the very throne of God. It is their scintillating brilliancy which glorifies the visions of both Ezekiel and Isaiah, and which they described as revolving wheel within wheels, revealing ever new and wider vistas of supernal glory.

St. Martin, writing on the subject of mystic numerology, says: "The number Four is that without which nothing can be known as it is the universal number of perfection. The Supreme Cause; although connecting with the source of all numbers, proclaims itself especially by the number of the square, which is at the same time the number of man. By reason of the divine virtue in this number he has a direct action on all septenary beings, and it recalls the eminent rank which he has occupied in his origin. From this we are given to understand that 4 belongs properly to the Logos, the word that was in the Beginning, or in other words, to the World of Creation.

In the Fourth Day of Creation the dual power was born which is represented by the Sun and the Moon in the sevenfold creative processes. Four and Seven are related to what has gone on before, and also to that which is to follow. Standing as they do between 1 and 10, the alpha and omega, the beginning and the end, they have been characterized by students of this sacred science as divine Numbers.

Pythagoras taught that 3 represents spirit, 4 signifies soul and 7 indicates awakened, responsible man.

From the Holy Four, the Great Nameless Ones, the Lords of Destiny, symbolized throughout the Bible by the Lion, the Eagle, the Ox, and the Man, and correlated astrologically with the Lords of the Fixed Signs, Leo, Aquarius, Taurus and Scorpio, emanated the initial spiritual forces which later crystallized upon the earth in the form of the four elements of which all material things are composed, namely fire, air, water and earth. The visions of biblical seers were observed in that exalted state of consciousness which we refer to as Initiation, and which they have recorded for our enlightenment and inspiration, are descriptions of the cosmic processes of creation. From this high place of cosmic knowing comes the chant: "The Four from the One and the Seven from the Four." As previously observed, the *Word*, by which all things are made, represents the four forces designated as Fire, Air, Water and Earth.

In the sevenfold vehicle of man, these four primary forces work in and through their correlated principles. Fire is linked to the desire nature; air to the mind; water to the emotions, and earth to the physical body.

The gradual refinement of these elements within man constitutes the regenerative process. It is what Paul describes as putting off the carnal and puttng on of the celestial. It is a sevenfold process and its result is the awakened and illumined Four.

"The Fourfold spiritual powers of the four elements became the fourfold mind power which gives Eternal Life as symbolized by the cabalistic wheels of fire, the chariot of Elijah."

Again drawing on Franz Hartmann, we read: "Try to find

the secret signification of the number Four which is alluded to
so frequently in the allegories of both the Old and New
Testaments. The number 40 is also frequent in the Bible.
Everything consists fundamentally of four elements, they
produce three Beginnings and from these originate the two
sexes, the Sun and the Moon, but the latter two produce the
Son, the mortal and divine man."

The work of the Fourth Creative Day as recorded in Genesis
is, as previously observed, connected with the formation of the
Sun and the Moon.

The above quotation of Franz Hartmann is descriptive in
part also of the profound significance of the mystic, magic
"Lost Word" of the Old Testament, Yod-He-Vau-He. It is the "I
am that I am" which was given to Moses as the supreme
talisman of power and authority. This magic soul word is
representative of the four elements. Yod correlates to Fire; He,
to Water; Vau, to Air, and the final He, which is feminine, to
Earth. From the Fire (Sun) and the Water (Moon), the Air (Son)
is produced.

It is on the earth which is the focussing point of the Ego in
its concentrated redemptive work upon this material plane. To
redeem matter and elevate it to a higher condition is the great
task which necessitates the cycles of reincarnation upon this
plane. It is only as the awakened spirit learns to redeem the
fallen Eve or "He" principle within himself that he comes into
possession of that Messianic or Christed power of the I am
which enabled Moses to overcome the obstacles he encountered
when leading the children of Israel to the
entrance of the Promised Land of the New
Day and Age.

Yod

He ————— He

Vau

In the hidden meanings of the accompanying
figure, the Tetragrammaton, carrying the
powerful four-lettered name, Yod-He-Vau-He,
is indicated the path of evolution for the masses, and also the

way of the few who choose the more direct path of Initiation. It also reveals the four elements of which the body of the earth and all things upon it are composed, thus correlating it with the work of the Fourth Day. We may also discover in this same design the cross of matter until the great transmutation processes have been completed and man is resurrected into a new and more perfect day. From these considerations of the Tetragrammaton we may surmise something of the reverence with which even the uninitiated regarded the Holy Name, Yod-He-Vau-He, and why it was never pronounced in public. One who understands its proper intonation can, by its use, effect marvellous transformations within himself, his environment, and all things within his radius. Such a knowledge, together with the power it gives its possessor, does not come to one until proven entirely selfless and dedicated wholly in service to the powers of Good. It was only the High Priest that was permitted to exercise this power in the Holy of Holies, and furthermore, the times were restricted to the nights of the full Moon. It was then that the High Servant of the Lord pronounced the magic word as blessing and benediction upon his people for the ensuing month. It was after his initiation into the use of this high power of the "I am that I am", that Moses was enabled to talk with God as a man speaks with a friend, and to ascend Mount Nebo, the Mount of Wisdom, there to be translated into the glories of the Life Everlasting.

Is-Is, the four-lettered "Lost Word" of the Egyptians, here the same mystic power for the Wise Men of the Egyptian Temples. These spiritual forces are latent within all men, and they will become active as we enter into the fourth dimensional consciousness of the new Aquarian Age. In the New Age about to be ushered in, the present Law of the Triad will be succeeded by that of the Tetrad, and the mysteries and the glories of the inner worlds will be revealed. It is in this new, glad Day that death will be no more, that God will wipe away all tears for the former things (the three dimensional consciousness) will have passed away.

In all Mystery Schools, the development of the fourth dimensional consciousness has been connected with the Fourth Degree or Step of Enlightenment. It is correlated with what is spoken of as the formation of the Sun and Moon. In this Fourth Step the mystic Mason will find again the Lost Word of his Craft.

The symbol of Four is a Star, and its most important color is blue, the color of spirit. In the transmutation or cleansing and redemptive processes which constitute the supreme work of 4, we find that it becomes also the number of ripe fate, or the liquidating of present destiny. Hence the frequent use of the "40 year" period in the stories of the Bible. Forty, which is a higher power of 4, is the number under which debts are paid off. Many of the most prominent biblical characters passed through a probationary period of 40 years or 40 days, even the great Christ himself "anhungered 40 days." This same period of reparation is retained even today in the modern church in the Lenten Season observances. Such an interlude of 40 does not necessarily consist of exactly so many days or years, but has reference primarily to the regenerative powers of 4 as these manifest on all planes of being - physical, emotional, mental, and spiritual. Four is the magic wand of Transformation.

A 4 person is born for new opportunities. This physical incarnation opens for him the door that leads to different and larger spheres of knowing and becoming. If the nativity is centered in material living, the new experiences may come through worldly success and the accumulation of earthly possessions. If, on the other hand, the Ego is ready for a spiritual awakening, as is often true of a 4, the following words may find literal fulfillment: "After this, I looked and behold, a door was opened in Heaven." The third dimensional consciousness is expanded 'into that of the fourth dimension; the wonders and glories of realms hitherto invisible are revealed before the enchanted vision of the newly illumined one. He finds himself called into new and wider fields of service; he has qualified for that high and noble calling of conscious invisible helpership.

A marked characteristic of the Four person who functions largely in the material sphere of life, is self will that is so determined that it expresses itself as a decided stubbornness, tenaciousness, and an extreme sensitiveness.

Equally pronounced characteristics of a spiritually awakened Four are understanding, sympathy, and compassion that extends to all things, and a developed intuition that is truly the voice of the spirit within. The Four is wise if he heeds the voice of this inner monitor. He will come to learn that he is never mistaken when he does so, and as he follows this guidance from within ever more closely, he enters into an ever fuller realization that the voice of the spirit ever rings true. The one who understands these things gains both physically and spiritually when he learns to go daily into "his closet and there pray to his Father in secret." He will find a verbatim fulfillment of the promise: "His Father which is in secret will reward him openly." It was from the heights (in consciousness) of this secret place, or inner shrine, that Solomon gained both understanding and the wisdom that placed him among the greatest of Initiate-kings, and which made him an illustrious example of that to which a Four may aspire and to which he may ultimately attain.

One, Two and Three in their triadic emanations are largely masculine; Four, Five, and Six in their triadic emanations are pronouncedly feminine. Four, therefore, is more successful and finds the largest sphere of usefulness in activities which are set in feminine rhythms of beauty and artistry, or in following those pursuits which are of some humanitarian or altruistic endeavor and require the exercise of feminine qualifications such as intuitive perception, tact, tenderness, sympathy and compassion.

Four opens a new doorway in the life that may lead to heights illimitable, to far vistas as yet unperceived, or to paths of psychic disillusionment. Four, in its highest aspects, voices the love tones of the awakened Christ within when He says: "Behold, I stand at the door and knock; if you will open for me, I will come in and abide with you."

KEY THOUGHTS

"They that venerate the number Four do not ill to teach that by reason of this number everybody has its origin."

As the Divine Spirit descends into physical incarnation, new forces are brought into manifestation, some possessing a masculine potency and others, a feminine.

QUESTIONS ON LESSON FOUR

1. What part in this evolutionary scheme is denoted by 4?
2. What correlation can you find between 4 and the 4th Zodiac
3. What biblical character is attuned to 4 besides those referred to in this lesson?
4. Give some keyword descriptive of 4.

NOTE: These lessons are not intended for casual reading, but for careful study and meditation wherein it is hoped that by a lifting of consciousness the student may be able to contact the inner man — that source of light eternal which makes life complete both within and without.

THE NUMBER FIVE

> Five-Ten are regarded as the sign manual of
> height, depth, east, west, north, and south,
> forming the six sides of the cube and
> representing the idea of form in its geometrical
> perfection. — *Theosophical Arithmetic*

Five stands for the Christ, or the spirit, resurrected from the tomb of matter. Four is the cross upon which 1 is crucified. Only as the lower nature is subjugated or crucified does the ego begin to rise toward freedom through a recognition of its innate divinity.

It is in accordance with these facts that the esoteric numerology of the early Christians held five to signify the sacred wounds upon the body of Christ Jesus, these being 5 in number. Related to this fact is the sorrow of the Via Dolorosa; since this is so difficult and beset with so many temptations, the number 5 has been considered by some to be a portent of evil. In the numerical mysticism of St. Martin, the quinary is the number of evil principle. However, earlier systems of numerology gave 5 as the number of macrocosm. If, then, we consider 5 representative of man's attempt to rise above the chaos of the present age, we can see where the difficulties involved in such an accomplishment would be looked upon as unfortunate, or evil from the personal point of view, whereas in reality, from the viewpoint of the spirit and its progress it merely identifies with the severe trials inevitably encountered in attaining to the state of eternal good, Five is good in the making.

The life and works of the apostle Paul are indicative of the powers of 5. Says Paul: "It doth not yet appear what we shall be." These words are particularly applicable to 5, the true symbol of which is the Pentagram, the five pointed star. Five has been called the dual number because it represents the two natures, the higher and the lower, which contend for supremacy in the life of man. The victory of the higher or spiritual nature over the lower is beautifully illustrated in the life of Paul, the change resulting in the adoption of another name, Saul, which became Paul, the former name representing in his case the lower man. In his awakened spiritual state he could no longer endure the vibratory impacts of the name Saul. The letter 'P' or 'Phe' in Hebrew, is symbolical of light, and is represented pictorially by a star.

In the struggle between the two conflicting natures, the person coming under 5 must contend with a nervous, restless energy. His environment undergoes constant change. Life being his supreme teacher, he is brought into touch with many places, personalities, and problems, each and all of which yield their quota of experience and supply an abundance of material out of which to extract the qualities that make for wisdom, character, and the growth of the soul.

Since 5 is half of 10, the cycle of unity, it is not surprising to find the 5 person a wide traveler. But his wanderings are not aimless; they contribute to the enrichment of the spirit and the strength of will and purpose necessary to meet successfully the trying situations which invariably meet the pilgrim on the path of 5.

The Masonic Fraternity is instructed that 5 is the most important number because it is at the center of the series of 10 which embraces unity. Two paths are continuously opening for the Five. Situations appear to reappear which represents the choice between the high and the low. Five is a powerful number for good or ill.

The pentagram, which is the symbol of 5, represents man with arms and legs outstretched and head erect. It is the 1 resurrected from out of the tomb or cross of matter. So we may say 1, 2, 3, 4 and 5 represent the human series. They are the powers under which mankind has attained to its present state of consciousness. The numbers 6, 7, 8, and 9 point the way over which humanity may attain to complete emancipation and final atonement with divinity. That consummation is realized in 10, or unity, which marks the end of a numerical series and the conclusion of the present cycle of manifestation.

The crucial, decisive point in life experience marked by 5 links it closely in parable and allegory with 7, the number of earth work completion. The Supreme Master gave His disciples a beautiful lesson in the spiritual significance of numbers in the Parable of the Loaves and Fishes. There were to commence with, 5 loaves and 2 fishes, yet, after the multitude had been fed, there remained *twelve* baskets full of food. Five is a pendulum swinging between the influence of 2, the imperfect, and 3, the perfect. The Loaves and Fishes of the Christ parable are symbols of the essences of life which are extracted out of the experiences encountered in the course of our successive cycles of earth life. In terms of the Parable, the spiritual powers of 5 have lifted the powers of 2 above duality to the higher level whereon polarity is realized, the 5 and the 2 equalling the 7 through which the creative powers brought the world into being. The Days of Creation number 7. The result of this operation produces 12 − hence, in the Parable 12 baskets full remained. It indicates the far-reaching influences of the individual who has attained to the powers of 12. Twelve holds 3, the first perfect number, as its digit.

Before it was possible for Joshua, the foremost disciple of Moses, to perform the magical feat of causing the Sun and Moon to stand still, which is but another expression of bringing duality into equilibrium, he was compelled to war upon and subjugate five kings. It was only after this important experience, which was the turning point in his life, that he was able to enter into the Promised Land (New Age). Melchizedek, priest and mystic, met the five kings in battle, and not until he had vanquished these did he bestow the rites which we refer to as the Order of Melchizedek upon Abraham in the city of Salem, the high place of peace. The five kings symbolize in both instances the powers of the five senses which at present so largely dominate the life of man.

Both of the above cited Old Testament records pertaining to 5 bear much the same numerical significance as does that of the Parable of the Loaves and Fishes. In the New Testament instance the work of spiritual realization is carried farther than in the Old. The former strikes a higher evolutionary keynote, coming as it does under the regime of the Christ than the Old, which came under the direction of Jehovah.

In the Parable of the Loaves and Fishes, 5 has become

"The master of his fate, the captain of his soul."

Such a one is truly represented by the five-pointed star. He has gained that most desirable of all gifts, the power of self-control. Not the Heavens above, the elements beneath, nor the invisible forces everywhere present can cause him to swerve from the right. The star is his crown and he wears it gloriously, influencing all whom he contacts by the radiance of its light. Such is the high destiny of 5 as revealed by biblical sages who knew its highest functions.

Five is the star; its color is a sheer luminous pink; and its highest status is represented by the sage. (The word 'sage' carries the power of 4).

The following lines are excerpts from the Pythagorean writings concerning the number 5:

> Five is eminently a spherical and circular number because in every multiplication it restores itself, and is found terminating the number; it is change of quality, because it changes what has three dimensions into the sameness of a

sphere by moving circularly and producing light, and hence light is referred to the number Five.

Five is the "privation of strife" because it unites in friendship the two forms of the numbers, even and odd, the 2 and the 3.

Five is Venus, which unites the male Three and the female Two. It is also a demi-goddess, because it is half of the decad, which is Divinity. Also Pallas the immortal, because Pallas presides over the ether, or the fifth element which is indestructible and is not material to our present senses.

Five is Cardiatis, or Cordelia, because like a heart, it is in the middle of the body of the nine digits when placed thus:

$$1\ 2\ 3$$
$$4\ 5\ 6$$
$$7\ 8\ 9$$

It is interesting to note in connection with the last item mentioned above that 5 is Leo, the fifth sign of the zodiac which governs the heart.

The vowels of a language are the centers or foci of spiritual forces. In Oriental theology as presented in the most ancient stanzas of the Vedas it is taught that it was through these forces that Brahma created the world. In the wisdom of the ancient Hebrews it was held that the five vowels were centers of good or evil, avenues of white or black magic, in accordance with the manner inwhich they were used. In ancient Greece the five vowels hung upon the walls of the Delphic temple, presenting to the neophyte who came to inquire into the Mysteries and opportunity for proving their qualifications for admission and advancement through deciphering their spiritual significance. Five was proclaimed the sacred number of this temple.

The vowels are feminine, and in a name they represent the nature and strength of the forces that incline toward a knowledge of the secrets of nature and a practice of the mystical truths of life not even recognized as yet by the masses of humanity. The vowels are the hidden sanctuary within wherein dwell the highest aspirations and the holiest impulses of the soul; they constitute the Holy of Holies which no alien presence ever desecrates. It was of this sanctuary of the spirit that Emerson wrote when he said: "All men descend to meet." In this same high place abide the noble impulses and the lofty dreams that are destined to come some time or other to birth in the waking consciousness of evolving man, and to place their celestial signature indelibly upon the personal life of the external man.

Five is the number of joy and sorrow; the two qualities between which a Five oscillates until the opposites have been reconciled into a higher polarity.

It is the purpose of this course of Numbers to aid the student to recognize the highest power of each number and to point the way to an effective cooperation with these powers. There is available to us in this science of vibration a knowledge of laws by which we can release more fully and speedily the latent idealism within our inmost natures and come to live ever more fully in harmony with universal principles of good. By accentuating the highest spiritual qualities of numbers we hope to assist the students of this Divine Science to approach the subject with reverence and devotion, and to live in accordance with its sacred precepts,

The Parable of the Pounds

A certain nobleman went into a far country to receive for himself a kingdom, and to return, And he called ten servants of his and gave them ten pounds, and said unto them trade ye herewith till I come. But his citizens hated

him, and sent a message after him saying, we will not that
this man reign over us.

And it came to pass, when he was come back again,
having received the kingdom, that he commanded his
servants, unto whom he had given the money, be called
to him, that he might know what they had gained by
trading. And the first came before him saying, Lord, thy
pound hath made ten pounds more. And he said unto
him, Well done, thou good servant; because thou was
found faithful in a very little, have thou authority over
ten cities. And the second came, saying, Thy pound,
Lord, hath made five pounds. And he said unto him also,
Be thou also over five cities.   *– Luke 19:12-19*

In esoteric symbology a city denotes a state of
consciousness, and it is with the development of consciousness
in some one or another of its many aspects that the Master is
chiefly concerned in the several parables attributed to Him. In
the unfoldment of consciousness lies the key to the secret of
spiritual development.

Five represents the awakening of the "I AM" within, the
dawning realization of God in Man. In its highest relationships,
Five sees in retrospect the path of its evolution from the time
that it first contacted matter while yet in spirit at the stage of 1
up to its present individualized and illumined status as a true
messenger of the gods, ready to receive the commandment
which is given only to one who has attained self-mastery: "Be
thou also over five cities". The Five also looks into the future
beholding an ever-ascending spiritual development that leads
finally to a complete at-one-ment with spirit. At this stage he
will hear the commendation: "Well done, thou good servant.
Because thou was found faithful in a very little have thou
authority over ten cities".

Five is the keystone in the arch of the structure of life; in
the series of 9, four numbers are on each side. A Five person

will meet in life a series of situations in which he is called upon to make a definite choice. In the last analysis that choice is one that calls for allegiance to the forces of construction and progression or an adherence to the powers of negation and retrogression. The perfect ideal for the Five was given by the Christ in the five words which shone upon His robe at the time of the Transfiguration like five scintillating stars, i.e., "Glorious robe of my strength."

In Daniel we read: "Unto two thousand and three hundred days, then shall the sanctuary be cleansed." The sanctuary referred to is the huma body, the living temple of the indwelling God. The supreme work of 5, as Daniel states, is the cleansing of the sanctuary, or the regeneration of the body of man.

In Matthew we find further instruction as to the process of renewal or redemption:

The Parable of the Ten Virgins

Then shall the kingdom of heaven be likened unto ten virgins, who took their lamps, and went forth to meet the bridegroom. And five of them were foolish, and five were wise. For the foolish, when they took their lamps, took no oil with them; but the wise took oil in their vessels with their lamps. Now while the bridegroom tarried, they all slumbered and slept.

But at midnight there is a cry, Behold the bridegroom! Come ye forth and meet him. Then all those virgins arose, and trimmed their lamps. And the foolish said unto the wise, Give us of your oil, for our lamps are going out. But the wise answered, saying, Peradventure there will not be enough for us and you; go ye rather to them that sell, and buy for yourselves.

And while they went away to buy, the bridegroom came, and they that were ready went in with him to the marriage feast; and the door was shut. Afterward came

also the other virgins, saying, Lord, Lord, open to us. But
he answered and said, Verily, I say unto you, I know you
not. Watch therefore, for ye know not the day nor the
hour.   *– Matt. 25:1-13*

The bridegroom symbolizes the Christed powers of the
illumined five, the five wise virgins. The marriage refers to the
union of the head and heart, or intellect and intuition. This
blending produces an inner illumination which is maintained by
the oil of the soul, or wisdom, and this inner luminosity
produces an expansion of the five senses so that the virgins
become truly 'wise'. The parable also indicates the dual path
before which the Five must make his choice.

The number 365 digits 5. It is the numerical value of the
days making up the cycle of the calendar year, a period of
opportunities for progress and for the harvesting of fruits grown
from seeds previously planted.

Five is essentially the number of life. A Five lives to the
fullest in this physical expression; he almost automatically
extracts the very essence of every experience which life holds
for him. There are no halfway measures he aims to enter fully
into the entire gamut of experience, and will let go of none
until he has explored it in its entirety.

The fifth letter of the Hebrew alphabet is He or H, the Hota
of the ancient Greek. This letter also means life or vitality; it
refers not only to physical animation, but to the capacity for
breathing a more rarefied air than that known to the average
mortal.

When the Five has learned the lessons that physical
experience has to teach him, he is ready to experience this
inflow from on high which will make him a new and different
being. Such was the transformation that occurred in the lives of
Abraham and Sarah with the addition of the letter "H" to their
names. This transformation has a meaning for both the inner
and the outer life. It manifests physically as exuberant health

and expresses itself intellectually in an increasingly sensitized and enriched mind which in turn becomes instrumental through its well-focussed and controlled powers to reflect more fully and accurately the faculties of the spirit within. Those double effects occurred in the lives of both Sarah and Abraham after the addition of "H"(5) to their names. True to the nature of the change as this may be known in the light of the science of numerical emanation, a new joy (Isaac) was born to the renewed lives of the patriarchal couple. It is only after such a new birth that one is really alive.

Paul referred repeatedly to this transition in consciousness as "putting off the old and putting on the new." Such is the work of 5. It is a tremendous change, and before it can be effected there must be a reversal in the flow of the life process. Whereas they are now directed chiefly outward and downward, they must be turned inward and upward. Regeneration is particularly the work of 5 as evidenced in the life and divine apostleship of Paul.

The word 'corn' which is used so frequently in both the Old and the New Testaments, is a 5-power word, and has reference in this specific regenerative process. In this connection study the account given in Genesis of the famine that occurred when Joseph was Prime Minister of Egypt, and the multitudes that came into that land in search of the needed corn. The Five makes this journey into Egypt many times before he is finally successful in obtaining his portion of the coveted grain. When he does receive his measure of corn, he realizes what occurred in the life of Paul on his journey.

The fifth element is Mercury. It is Quintessence, or the substance of all things. To synthesize, refine, and spiritualize all experience into the oil of soul wisdom for keeping eternally alight the lamps of the Wise Virgins is the destiny of 5.

KEY THOUGHTS

"The number 5 appears in the Scriptures most often in two relations, i.e., the planes of manifestation and the senses."

Some of the forces contacted by the Ego are harmonious, others inharmonious, the purpose of evolution being to transform darkness into light, matter into spirit, and death into eternal life.

QUESTIONS ON LESSON FIVE

1. What part of this evolutionary drama is represented by 5?
2. Correlate 5 with the fifth zodiacal sign, Leo.
3. What biblical character typifies the forces of 5?
4. Give some keywords descriptive of 5.

Now in the sixth month, of Elizabeth, the angel
Gabriel was sent from God unto Nazareth to a
virgin, and the virgin's name was Mary.
                                        – Luke 1:26,27.

In East Indian theology, Siva △ represents the principle
of Fire; Vishnu ▽ the principle of Water. When the upright
and the inverted triangles are interlaced they form what is called
Solomon's Seal. This same figure is also called the Philosopher's
Diamond. A remembrance of this fact will help us to understand
something of the inner meanings contained in the following
words by Rabbi Abba; "We are all six lights shining forth from a
seventh. The great work is to unite the sixth to the seventh."

The number 6 is essentially a working, building number. The
work of creation was completed in six days. The Book of
Genesis which contains the creation account, is keyed to 6. The
Chinese say: "Six Breaths produced all things in silence."
Jeremiah, one of the principal workers and builders for the New
Age new dawning, also responded to the vibratory rhythms of 6.

Six pertains to the interrelationship of the human and the
divine. In the power of 6 the human and the divine meet but
not as a result of the divine descending to the human as it does
under the power of 1, bt through an elevation of the human to
the higher levels of the divine. Since, then, the association of the
human and the divine is dependent upon the upliftment of the
former, the number 6 is one of preparation through purification.

Six is a feminine number. It was dedicated by Pythagoras to
Venus, the goddess of human love. It is through the sorrows
growing out of personal love that the soul awakens to the new

and the higher life which lead to resurrection or illumination. From the sixth to the ninth hours, the face of the earth was darkened as the Master agonized upon the cross in his great service for humanity. The work which the Six must undertake, that is, the experiences through which he must pass, in order to learn all the lessons of his numerical mentor, will result in a soul radiance, a light such as "never yet lay on land or sea." St. Martin says that six should not be regarded so much as a separate and active number, but rather as an eternal law impressed upon all numbers. It is only in the light of the foregoing that we can fully understand this statement of Martin.

Six belongs to Venus and bears the signature of Beauty. It belongs to the soul quality which results from a blending of justice and mercy. The latter are products of a life that has experienced alternating light and shadow, and that has interwoven the forces of man with those of God. The human and the divine are brought into a working partnership.

It is the feminine potency in man (represented by 6) which is the motive power of redemption. In harmony with this fact, 6 bears the characteristics of the Cosmic Mother which is identified astrologically as Virgo, the sixth sign of the Zodiac. The color belonging to 6 is heliotrope, a color rendered luminous through suffering.

The beautiful idyl of Ruth and Boaz offers a helpful study of the number 6. We read in the Book of Ruth, 3:15: "Bring the mantle that is upon thee, and hold it; and she held it; and he measured six measures of barley and laid it on her." It was only after the period of preparatory work, symbolized by the six sheaves of barley, had been accomplished, that Ruth was ready for the rites of the mystic marriage. It is also interesting to note in this connection that barley symbolizes purity, and that it is, moreover, associated with Virgo or the Virgin.

In Egypt, the Lunar Sabbath was celebrated on the sixth day. Osiris was called the Lord of the Sixth Day Festival. The rites were concerned with the opening of the sacred eye which occurred onthe sixth day. It was also on the sixth day that the Annunciation came to the Blessed Virgin. In many lands the sixth day has been observed by some religious festival in honor of the powers and offices of motherhood.

The Pythagoreans assigned to 6 the perfections of all parts. The reason for this arises from the fact that the number is formed by the multiplication of 3, the first odd number beyond 1 or unity, and the first even number. It signifies the union of male and female in generation. Hence 6 has been associated by many numerologists with the forces of sex or generation.

The early Christians taught that 6 represented sex or sin. Since chastity was with thema fundamental teaching, the words were normally interchangeable and synonomous and represented the same thing.

The vibratory powers of every number express themselves on higher and lower levels according to the development of the individual coming under their special influence. A Six person passes through the lower cycles of his number's nature before responding to its highest values. In the earlier stages of development, the tendency is to abuse rather than to rightly use the holy creative life force. But at length through sorrow and suffering the lesson of conservation and transmutation is learned. The Six in its highest aspects is exemplifed in the love idyl of Ruth and Boaz. It is also expressed in the exquisite portrayal with which John the Divine opens his Gospel; it is to be noted, too, in the wedding feast at Cana in Galilee where the Christ transformed 6 pots of water into the luminous wine of immortality. It is in the light of this high, sacred meaning of 6 that we may understand that ancient reference to this number which says: "There is but one perfect number between One and Two and that is Six."

Cosmically 6 is a commingling of the "three Philosophical Fires and the three Philosophical Waters from whence comes the procreation of the elements and all things." Biblically this is the work of the sixth Creative Day which is described thus: "God created man in His own image, in the image of God created He him, male and female created He them. And God saw everything He had made, and behold it was very good. And the evening and the morning were the sixth day." (Gen. 1:27,31.)

At its highest, 6 is the unknowable in man. It is the urge of this unknown divine factor within man that gradually expands his consciousness until it rises to heights of majesty and glory, where it can declare with St. Paul: I was caught up into the third heaven and there saw wonders which it is not lawful for me to reveal." The Book of Revelation also throws light on the inner significance of 6. Four Recording Angels surround the Throne, each of which possesses six wings. The adoring elders that surround the Throne are four and twenty in number, 4 and 2 and 0 giving the value of 6. Thus we find the operations of 6 in the creative processes on the physical plane as recorded in the creation story of Genesis and also on the higher spiritual planes as revealed to John in his beatific vision on the Isle of Patmos.

The esoteric orientalists know well the tremendous potency resident in numbers and from Tibet have come some powerful incantations which, rightly used, could change the lives of individuals. When employed by an adept they are capable of producing sweeping transformations in an entire nation. These magic formulas or incantations have been composed of *six syllables*.

In that supreme treatise of magic and mysticism, the Book of Revelation, power was given the beast that he might become dominant upon the earth for forty and two months. Again the number 6. This period of three and one half years, it may also be noted, is one half the cycle of 7. Six is the power that is active beneath the surface, the force within which is incessantly striving for attainment and completion. This is equally true whether the force be directed to good or evil objectives.

The Lord Christ was manifest in the Master Jesus for a period of 42 (6) months. King David, founder of the House of Israel, reigned in Jerusalem the great City of Peace, for 33 (6) years. During that time the creative powers of 6 were manifest in Jerusalem as never before, and the Holy City became a center of such beauty and magnificence that it attracted the attention and admiration of the world.

The highest degree conferred by Freemasonry is the honorary 33 degree. The true Mason who lives up to the full significance of this exalted degree enters upon the inner path of six, whereon sex force is transmuted into higher powers such as enable him to travel in foreign lands and visit the mystic city of Jerusalem, there to know the powers of a true ascended master.

Within the wondrous and intricate organism of man there are 33 (6) vertebrae protecting the spinal canal through which the transmuted life forces pass from the lower generative center to the higher faculties in the head. This vertebral column with its 33 "steps" is the Ladder of Jacob. On it the aspirant climbs to heavenly heights where he, too, may exclaim with the patriarch of old: "Surely this is God's house and I knew it not."

Some savants have taught that a World Teacher appears every 600 years for the purpose of furthering the emancipation of mankind and restoring the earth to its Edenic state of purity and spiritual well-being.

The interlaced triangle, as previously observed, represents the powers of 6, as these descend from the divine into the human. The swastika, also a symbol of 6, is a cosmic glyph of all things that are and are to come. It indicates the dynamic urge to become reunited with the higher self. This urge lies back of all spiritual legend, allegory, and parable, and testifies to the ceaseless activity of 6.

The significance of the swastika is similar to that of the mallet in Freemasonry. It is an instrument by which something may be beaten or whipped into a new form. Biblically it is expressed as the separation of "the real from the unreal, the false from the true." The illumined six lives in rhythms that bring forth the new. Its spirit is voiced by Oliver Wendell Holmes when he utters the exhortation: "Build thee more stately mansions, O my soul."

No teacher has ever taught more beautifully or more decisively of the numbers in relation to human life than did the Master Himself. The Parable of the Laborers; Matthew, twentieth chapter, is recommended to the student for careful meditation. In this parable the Master deals with the spiritual operation of the numbers 3, 6, 9, and 11 in their relation to human life, the primary urge of each being a return to unity, an atonement with the divine. The "wages" for which the laborers worked were 1. Three is the first perfect number and has to do with the upliftment of spirit, soul, and body. Six signifies beauty and harmony established throughthe magnetic law of equilibrium. This is represented in the Kaballah as Tipherath, the light which shineth no longer in the darkness. It is the light which comes with the attainment realized during the "mystic span of 33 years" previously mentioned. Nine trebles the forces of 3; under that triune power the three principles of man comprising the body, the soul, and the spirit, are united into a single functioning unit. Each of these three principles is triune in its nature. The threefold body (physical, etheric, and astral) is joined to the three-aspected spirit (created in the likeness of the triune God), and these united trinities bring into being the soul, the essence of experience garnered by the spirit when incarnate in form and this soul is also of a threefold power corresponding with the two trinities of body and spirit from the coupled activities of which it comes into being. Ultimately the 3 plus 3 powers of body and soul will be absorbed by the threefold spirit which will then possess the powers of 3 plus 3 plus 3 or 9. In these facts we have the reason for considering 9 the number both of humanity and of Initiation.

Eleven is the signpost of Mastership, the activity in whom the work described has been consummated. Eleven works well spiritually with numbers specified in connection with that work. Astrologically these numbers correlate with Gemini (3), Virgo (6), Sagittarius (9), and Aquarius (11). These signs, like their related numbers, represent definite principles in he body of the macrocosmic Man, and steps which lead to Mastership and the New Age of equality and unity.

In Genesis, 6 is working for the illumination which it attains in the Parable of the Laborers in Matthew's Gospel. In its highest aspects, 6 guards with brooding wings of beauty and harmony the Throne Eternal of the Supreme Power of Love.

A Six person finds his best working opportunities derived from a partnership with one of the opposite sex. Six is fundamentally a subjective worker, and a close association with one of an opposite polarity proves advantageous from the viewpoint of both the inner and the outer life.

In the life experience of a highly spiritualized Six, such a partnership relation with one of the opposite sex is not essential because the soul emanation of Six is masculine-feminine; it embraces the blended forces of both the Sun and the Moon. This high state of development is most aptly represented by the Sun-clothed woman of Revelation standing with her feet upon the Moon.

The vibratory rate of the cosmic force which impresses the powers of 6 upon any form of creation, proclaims the fact that the evolution of form is perfected, and that henceforth it is the urge of spirit that becomes paramount. God always sees that the work of the sixth day is good and a preparation for the "rest", or subjective interlude of the seventh. Therefore it follows naturally that a Six person does not usually succeed amid the objective activities of the world. He is more often the inner, the secretive, the secluded worker. Six will invariably, like Nicodemus, "come by night" to "display his wares' before his

Lord.

The inner workings of 6 are to be found throughout all nature in both the mineral and the flower kingdoms. In the Bible, two of the most widely used words, words concealing vast treasures in the hidden mysteries of Christ's teachings, are six-power words, namely, *wine* and *fish*. The word *Genesis*, which is with esoteric as well as academic appropriateness the name of the Sacred Book of Creation, is also a word bearing the impress of the forces that lie behind the number 6.

In the Tarot the sixth hieroglyph is called "The Lovers," and is represented by a young man standing between two female figures. One is crowned with the leaves of the vine, symbolic of sense intoxication; the other is crowned with flowers and represents wisdom. Every ego must choose which of these feminine attributes he will develop within himself, for Aphrodite or Minerva, the lower and the higher feminine within, are each struggling for recognition and conquest.

Six is feminine, subjective, formative, creative, Venusian. A Six year is a marrying year, a love year.

Six, in its personal aspects, invites to sexual excesses. In its spiritual attributes it points to the mystic Madonna of the Immaculate Conception. The ego is free to choose the path it would follow.

KEY THOUGHTS

"Through the various folk legends of the world, we find Six constantly recurring as the numerical exponent of perfection."

In the formation of numerals we may find a key to their symbolic meaning. Straight lines are masculine and spiritually aspiring. Curved lines are feminine and occult, mysterious.

QUESTIONS ON LESSON SIX

1. What do you find to be the signification of 6?
2. What is the relationship of 6 to the sixth sign of the zodiac, Virgo?
3. What biblical character is an exponent of the powers of 6?
4. Give some keywords descriptive of 6.

NOTE: These lessons are not intended for casual reading, but for careful study and meditation wherein it is hoped that by a lifting of consciousness, the student may be able to contact more fully the inner man, the source of wisdom and light eternal which makes life complete both within and without.

THE NUMBER SEVEN

> Seven they are; they are Seven. In the
> subterranean deep they are Seven. Perched in
> the sky they are Seven.
>> – *From an old Babylonian Fragment.*

Seven is the number possessing the deepest and most far reaching symbology of the entire fundamental series running from 1 to 10. It represents rest, completion. After the work of the 6 Creative Days, there follows the divine consummation of the whole in the seventh, the Sabbath or the Holy Day.

Seven is the number of spiritual realization and consummation. Each of the 7 Creative Days is attuned to the vibratory rate of a specific number. Could we observe in the Memory of Nature, the impress of these Seven Days, we would see that the rhythmic motion, the color, and the formation of each object and being in the processes of creation harmonized with the keynote of the Creative Day to which they belong. The keynote of each of the Creative Days is that of the planetary body to which it is attuned and by which it is ruled. It was in the light of this knowledge that Pythagoras declared that all the world is made by number.

> And God rested on the Seventh Day from all the work
> which He had made.

The Seventh Day "rest" does not refer to a cessation of activity but to the emergence from Chaos into a higher and a more perfect Order.

Herein, therefore, lies the true work of the 7. This number does not enter into the turmoil of experience in its inception but becomes operative when the time is ripe to establish new conditions and to supercede the old by a new and higher series. This is its function under every circumstance and condition, and it applies not only to personal relationships but equally to its activity in national and international affairs.

The powers of 7 will decide on what plane an individual's activities are centered. For numbers, like the zodiacal signs, possess degrees of vibration, each ego responding to that degree which accords with his evolutionary status.

Seven at his highest is the victor, the conqueror, the invincible and spiritual master. The seventh sephira on the kabalistic Tree of Life is "NETZACH", meaning victory, and the Tarot symbol for 7 is that of a king seated in a chariot and driving two sphinxes, one white, the other black. On his head the king wears a crown composed of three golden pentagrams, the latter being a symbol of man. Here we have a representation of the highest phase of 7 − body purified, mind illumined, and spirit glorified. The victor indeed, "resting" from his sevenfold labors and ready to extend his accumulated and strengthened forces in this "seven day" experience into new and wider fields of progress and endeavor.

'Septos', the Greek for 7, means holy, divine, motherless; it is the emanation of that supreme power which descends from on high. Minerva, springing full-armed from the head of Jove, is representative of the powers of 7.

Plato, in *Timaeus*, declares that the soul of the world was generated from 7. Other ancient sages described nature as a golden egg surrounded by 7 natural elements, 4 visible, and 3 invisible. The 4 visible elements were designated as air, water, fire, and earth.

All the principal religions and schools of spiritual development embody in their teachings and symbology the fundamental principle of the number 7. The values of 7 are divided into the trinity of·spirit and the quaternary of form. In spiritual science it is also taught quite universally that a sacred triad precedes the manifested 7, the 7 and 3 together constituting the perfect number 10.

Three, four, and seven, all bear a close relationship to each other; they are all powerful numbers of life, light, and union. The Trine typifies the spiritual and the Square the human. The union of the trine and the square signifies the interpenetration of the human and the divine. To realize such a union is the purpose of physical evolution. The process is embraced within the work of the seven creative days.

The sum of the first seven digits — 1,2,3,4,5,6,7, — equals 28. This number reduces to 10, the number of unity. The purpose of the cycles of earth lives is experience, and 7 marks the point in evolution when the gathered experience is synthesized and the resultant powers assembled for use as soul force. It was in keeping with this signficance of the number that the way to the Ancient Mystery Temples was marked by 7 steps, symbolic of 7 degrees. At the end of the "septenary discipline", the 4 has been transformed into the perfect square, the Tetragrammaton, and raised to a point of union with the trine of spirit. This is the force that is working through any sevenfold path in the number scope.

To the early Christians, 7 was representative of the gifts of the spirit, and in that sublime vision of John upon the mystic Isle of Patmos which is depicted in the *Book of Revelation*, 7 is its most important and emphatically accentuated number. John's *Apocalypse* consists of 7 visions, and the instrumentalities by which these visions were produced are likewise composed of 7 beings or objects. There are 7 retributive angels and 7 vials of wrath. Seven thunders utter their voices, and 7 angels open the 7 seals which release upon the earth the long accumulated karmic consequences of its past actions. Seven trumpets are sounded, and the scarlet woman of abomination rests upon the 7 hills.

The *Book of Revelation* recounts the ultimate triumph of good over evil, and the complete subjugation of the lower or negative forces by the positive or higher. Since this is the essential significance of 7, it becomes Saint John's chief numerical vehicle for conveying to man the truths beheld in his sevenfold vision as these are presented in the Mystery Book which concludes the Christian Bible.

It is written:

> When the 3 and the 4 kiss each other, then the cube unfolds and becomes the number of Life — the Father-Mother Seven.

The Secret Doctrine tells us that man is the septenary on the terrestrial plane of the One Great Unit (the Logos) which is itself the Seven-Vowelled sign, the Breath crystallized into the Word.

Seven may be considered the underlying keynote of nature because it governs the periodicity of all natural phenomena. There are 7 musical tones comprising the diatonic scale, 7 color rays constitute the visible spectrum, and 7 dominates the series of chemical elements. In cycles of a sevenfold rhythm is the human structure brought to completion. The first cycle of 7 deals with the physical building processes; the second cycle from 7 to 14 is marked by the development of feelings and emotions, the third cycle from 14 to 21 focusses the spiritual energy on the development of self will when the light of the spirit begins to dawn in the maturing consciousness. The period from 21 to 28 marks a most crucial period in that it brings a sort of recapitulation of the cycles preceding and also introduces the liquidation of causes generated in past lives. For this reason 28 is designated as the year marking the beginning of serious life. Thirty-three marks the synthesizing of the old and the beginning of the new. Thirty-five sees the fruition of the new, and 49, or 7 times 7, marks the climax of mental attainment.

The Bible account of the 7 lean years and the 7 full years

represents a specific formula in relation to the operation of spiritual law. This cyclic periodicity of 7 in the inner realms is reflected in a corresponding intervalin the motion, harmony, and rhythm of all being in manifestation.

"Three fell into Four in the lap of Maya".

All evolution, both secular and divine, moves in cycles of 7. This was the predominant number in the religions of both Babylon and Egypt. No ancient sage could boast of fame or fortune unless he bore some intimate connection with the number 7. It is the numerical power which is expressed by Jehovah. "Thou art the Seventh Light", chanted the priests in worship, and to which they added the affirmation that "we are the six lights which shine forth from the Seventh".

The mystery of 7 is concealed within that magical four-lettered Name of God with its threefold meaning, Yod-HeVau-He, or the Tetragrammaton. It is the "I am that I am" which became the prime motive power in the life and works of the great emancipator, Moses.

The I AM is the eternal and ever-existent principle of truth. Only as a man awakens this I AM consciousness within himself, is he able to contact truth in all things about him.

The 7 is introspective and intuitive; it is attracted to the unseen and mystic side of life and being. This is because the number is founded upon and centered in the very mystery of life and being. It embraces the "Four that are seen and the Three that are secret".

The name Je-ho-vah is composed of 7 letters and represents the foundation of the Christian religion. The letters J H V are symbols of the Trinity. The second H in the name represents the feminine, the love, or the Holy Ghost principle. It is the development of this principle that will constitute man's special spiritual work in he New Age now dawning. The 3 will then become 4.

"The Three fall into the Four. The Radiant Essence becomes Seven inside, Seven outside"

I AM is a 7 power word. A, or Aleph in Hebrew, is a masculine and a fire letter. M, or Mem, is a feminine and water letter. I, or Yod, is the ego, or the threefold spirit bound to the cross of matter, which is 4, and remains so until it discovers the way of freedom from bondage through its own inner illumination. Seven therefore, is the number of completion, of attainment, of rest — that complete rest which comes only after regeneration has been accomplished and the spirit emancipated from all that limits and binds. The state of illumination will then have been attained.

That the formative and creative processes of nature operate in the rhythm of 7 is substantiated in minerology. When the molecules of salt in solution begin to solidify, their first appearance is triangular or pyramidal and their second manifestation is that of a square or cube.

That the evolution of the present Fifth Root Race is attuned to the septenary keynote is instanced in the Noachic legend as recorded in the seventh chapter of Genesis: "Of every clean beast thou shalt take by seven . . . Of the fowls of the air by sevens. . . . For yet seven days, and I will cause it to rain upon the earth . . ."

Jehovah represents the threefold invisible spiritual essence by and through which all created things come into visible manifestation. Noah and his three sons, Shem, Japeth, and Ham, symbolize the fourfold or visible formations on the outer physical plane, and which are direct emanations from the hidden powers of the three-fold Godhead. Thus again we note the 4 proceeding from the 3 and producing the 7.

In the story of the Flood we read that when the waters receded, the ark rested on Mount Ararat. Note here the geometrical and the numerical patterns and their symbolical significance. The ark is represented by a square, the mount by a triangle.

The name 'Ararat' digits 4; the word 'ark', 3. In both instances Spirit (3) is represented as conjoined to matter (4). It is a symbol of Spirit entering into matter and thereby spiritualizing it. It is God moving upon the face of the waters for the purpose of creation. The motive power in the process is the union of the powers of 3 and 4.

The strange, lilting measures of the thirtieth chapter of Proverbs are set to the rhythm of seven.

Thus is the initial setting of the Fifth or Aryan Race attuned to the powers of 7. Hence it is that 7 possesses the ability to take precedence above all numbers in wresting the secrets of nature from their hiding places, whether these secrets belong to the scientific or the metaphysical world.

Zoology, embryology, and medicine, as well as the sciences of music and color, all attest to the workings of the septenary cycles upon the earth plane.

The Secret Doctrine states: "There is a harmony of number in all nature, in the force of gravity in the planetary movements, in the laws of heat, light, electricity and chemical affinity, in the forms of animals and plants, in the perception of the mind."

That the earth is attuned to the septenary rhythm is affirmed by the sevenfold vision of John as given in *Revelation*. The seven sacred Logoi by whom all creation proceeds and whom John names as the Seven Spirits before the Throne of God are reflected on this plane of manifestation in the sevenfold earth, the seven Root Races, the seven subraces, and the sevenfold body of man.

Pythagoras considered 7 to be the most sacred of all numbers and his students took their vows or obligations "by the number Seven".

The heavens also declare the glory of God in a septenary rhythm. In the constellations of both the Great and the Little

Bear are to be found 7 conspicuous stars. Orion has the same number. In Taurus are the seven Hyades, with the brilliant orange-yellow Aldebaran. Seven prominent lights are to be found in the Corona Borealis, the "God of the Shining Crown", as it was termed in Babylon. The mysticism of 7 is borne out also in the 7 sisters of the Pleadies, 6 of which are visible, the seventh being 'lost', which is to say, secret or concealed.

It was upon the rhythms of the octave that Pythagoras founded his cosmic harmonies called the music of the spheres. The distance from the earth to the moon was counted as one tone; From Mars to Jupiter, a half-tone; from Jupiter to Saturn, a half-tone; and from Saturn to the Zodiac, a tone — thus completing the full octave in celestial harmony. John in *Revelation* refers also to this heavenly chorus.

The 7 vowels, the feminine forces of speech, reflect the vibratory rhythms of these same astral keynotes. The moon is a most potent reflector of this seven-rayed power. Through each calendar month its forces are attuned to the influences of 7. Occult and mysterious, it sets its signature in sevens upon all evolving and manifesting forms.

Libra, the seventh of the zodiacal Hierarchies, marks the turning point between spirit and matter. It is, therefore, appropriately referred to as the Gate of the Gods. Libra is the symbol in the heavens of the Fall of Man and again of his redemption, when he shall become once more the perfected Adam Kadmon, the Heavenly Celibate of the Kaballah.

Seven is necessarily the principal number of the Bible. Its prevalent usage throughout the Old and the New Testaments is familiar to all students and so needs no detailed enumeration in this study. We note a single instance only, namely the *Book of Job*. Job was the father of 7 sons and 3 daughters. In the mysteries of the Yod, 10 entered the assembly and 7 came out. Job possessed 7000 sheep and 3000 cattle. His friends sat with him 7 days and nights and were commanded to sacrifice 7 bullocks and 7 rams. Eventually Job's 7 sons and 3 daughters were restored to him and he lived 140 years, or twice 7 times 10.

> For behold the stone that I have laid before Joshua; upon one stone shall be seven ages: behold, I will engrave the graving thereof, saith the Lord of hosts, and I will remove the iniquity of that land in one day.   *— Zachariah 3:9*

It is the Tincture of the 7 Sacred Logoi before the Throne of God termed the Philosopher's Stone, or Azoth by the alchemists, that the Wise Men of all time have learned to imbibe. This is the water of Eternal Life spoken of by the Master and which alone yields immortality. This same Tincture of the Logoi is the keynote of the Book of Zachariah. It is done to the rhythm of 7. It is also the power by which Peter became the stone upon which the church is built.

Seven is always preceded and succeeded by 7 because it represents an ever ascending series. Hence it must necessarily become the fundamental number of our present earth evolution which advances on a constantly ascending series toward the Sabbath Day of Perfection.

Pythagoras taught that "the soul is a number which moves of itself and contains the number four". The color of 7 is indigo. Its symbol is the triangle and the square, of the Masonic Apron. Both 3 and 4 were conceded to be symbols of profound and fruitful meditation in the Pythagorean school of Crotona. In this ancient seat of learning, instruction was given in much of the concealed wisdom of esoteric Masonry. The candidates were required to meditate on the occult powers of the triangle. Its first line, he learned, represented the mineral kingdom, the second the vegetable, and the third the animal.

This study belongs to a three dimensional world. On this plane man and woman are both incomplete and so desire perpetuation in issue. This desire is a manifestation of a subconscious longing for creation. When the soul learns to respond to the 4 of which Pythagoras teaches, man will no longer desire external creation. Marriage as an institution for the perpetuation of the race will yield to the mystic marriage such as the angels know on the higher plane of fourth dimensional consciousness. The perfect equilibrium of 4 will be realized as man-woman, woman-man. In the words of the Master, "I am in you, you are in me". Man becomes the Christed individual.

The triangular pyramid resting upon a cubical or square foundation is the cosmic symbol of 7. In terms of color it mainfests as purple. Here the full glory of the Tetragrammaton is revealed. The Sabbath Day of Rest is attained. The seven-brached candlestick of the Tabernacle represents the archtypal pattern of the earth and man. This pattern must be septenary so long as the labor is with 3 and 4.

KEY THOUGHTS

"Seven is a perfect number and signifies completion or consummation. It follows six which stands for completion of process."

The ego knows times of inbreathing and outbreathing, periods of rest and activity during its cyclic sweep of incarnations.

THE NUMBER EIGHT

"I praise Thee with my lips,
I know not the numbers."

Eight is a cosmic number. While that is true of all numbers, it is applicable to 8 in the sense that the vibratory power of 8 tends to lift one beyond the limitations of the personal environment. It is termed a 'free' number; also the resurrection number. Its color is light yellow, and carries the high powers of the Golden Christ Ray.

The birth force composes the working capital of a life, the substance of the rough ashlar which is to be fashioned into the perfect Cube. The keynote sounded by a name is the index of former achievements. Names are changed automatically as it were, as man touches higher levels of consciousness. It is an impossibility for the spirit to respond to the continuous vibrational impacts of a name which is inharmonious to its evolutionary status. Many names bestowed upon children are never used by them because they do not fit; others, in later years rename themselves. We cannot work with that which we do not understand. Nor is the spirit content to use that with which it has finished.

When Christenings come to be understood as being ceremonies of spiritual power attended even by the angels, an important step shall have been taken in the spiritual life of man. Because of the regenerative of 8, by far the greater number of the old fonts and baptistries are octagonal. In harmony with these facts we read in Luke 2:21:22:

> And when eight days were accomplished for the circumcising of the child, his name was called Jesus,

which was so named of the angel before he was conceived
in the womb, and when the days of his purification were
accomplished, they brought him to Jerusalem, to present
him to the Lord.

Eight is the highest feminine number of the entire series. It
is the number of the feminine in exaltation, referred to
sometimes by esoteric numerologists as the number of the
Double Feminine. In keeping with this signification it is the
symbol of awakened and developed soul faculties of the highest
type. An 8 is one in whom the still small voice ever speaks
clearly. It is the number of intuition par excellence.

The Book of Exodus is keyed to 8. The paramount message
of this Book is found in the words: "I was never disobedient to
the heavenly vision." These words are descriptive of 8. Those
who come under the rulership of this number rise easily above
the material and claim their own amidst the things of the
spiritual. Eight is the number of the resurrection into a higher
consciousness and a new manner of living. It is the power of the
divinity within which leads man, as represented by the children
of Israel, out of Egypt, the symbolical land of materiality ruled
over by Pharoah, the power of this world, and into a land
wherein they no longer function under bestial bondage but
under the laws of God. The highway of spirit is definitely
pointed out in this illuminating record of a God-guided people.
It outlines the steps on the path of soul attainment. It offers
truly an exodus from the old, the finite, and the personal, into
the Promised Land of the New Age, wherein freedom, equality,
soul comradeship and cosmic knowing, all of which are
key-words of 8, will be generally realized.

The study of external or objective nature is based upon the
four elements, carbon, hydrogen, nitrogen, and oxygen. These
four constituents pass through an extended or spiritual
gradation, also fourfold in number, but whose operations are

invisible to the outer physical plane senses. When man develops fourth dimensional consciousness, which gives the ability to observe, study, and tabulate something of the effects of these extended forces as they operate in their finer or more etheric gradations, he will be attuned to the true powers of 8 which now become his teacher as well as his servant, unveiling for him wonders which may not be lawfully revealed. These gradations of finer matter are known to the esotericists as Fire, Air, Water and Earth. In these forces are to be found the keys to inner plane development.

Moses, the primary personality of the Book of Exodus, is an 8 character. Pharaoh, the symbol of unregenerate man, is a 4. Four represents activity on the outer planes of materialism only. It embraces the realms of the material scientist whose world is bounded by the powers of oxygen, nitrogen, and carbon. Moses typifies the fourth dimensional consciousness wherein those fourfold forces are projected or lifted into the sphere of the 8.

This projection or expansion of faculties is difficult of accomplishment and is earned only by merit. The experiences encountered by the ego during this process of unfoldment are described briefly in the great Plagues of Exodus.

Through the multitude of external impacts experienced in the course of daily living the soul encounters joy and sorrow, pain and comfort, and all the many other opposites common to earth life. From these it makes an extract which becomes the spiritual substance out of which it builds the foundation stone upon which it fashions the New Age structure, namely, the consciousness that functions at will amid the glories of the new or Promised Land. This land is the true domain of the 8 who is born to know his cosmic heritage and who, for this reason, is obligated spiritually to aid all those who may ask for assistance. The 8 must always serve and point the way toward emancipation. For such service Moses is the ideal type.

The sublimated essences of initiatory experiences are

represented by Fire, Air, Water, and Earth. It is most interesting to note that the names of the Four Gospels which outline this fourfold Path leading to the Cosmic Temple of Light, collectively digit the number 8. Numerologically this indicates that in the Gospels is to be found the way of attainment and the supreme consummation of the high spiritual quest.

In a certain part of the Masonic Initiations the candidate is asked what he understands to be the meaning of the number 8. His answer: "This number is the sign of the Wise Men."

In order that we may have some comprehension of the inner wisdom which is concealed within this answer and at the same time be brought into a fuller realization of the cosmic significances of numbers and the primary importance that they hold in the continuously evolving scheme of life upon the earth planet, we shall turn in meditation to the primal symbolism of the number 8. Perhaps the most profound and far-reaching definition relative to the power, purpose and significance of number is: God is a number endowed with motion." The first initial impulses of God in creation are emblazoned upon the eternal Cosmic Records as specific lines of force or light forming the supreme Creative Fiat or Word, and in which all things are fashioned. These starry or spiritual patterns are in continuous and incessant motion and form the cosmic outline of the numerical series.

Each number is an accumulation of spiritual force or God power and is a mighty repository of God Immanent controlling a definite vibratory rhythm, or keynote, and emanating a certain specific color. Herein we find the very beginnings of the sacred science of numbers. They are God-Hieroglyphics, the writing of Deity upon the walls of Time and of Eternity, wherein "naught obtains its form but through the Deity, which is an effect of number."

Cosmically defined, motion and number are all but synonymous. At the heart of every atom is the number which sets the keynote of its rhythm or motion. The mystery of the octad, or 8, is that of the lemniscate, the eternal and continuous spiral motion which is the supreme signature of the universe and the path of all evolutionary cycles. The number 8 was first sounded by the alternate inbreathings and outbreathings of the planetary Earth Spirit. This cyclic motion of 8 appears in the caduceus, the staff of mystic wisdom carried by Mercury, or Hermes, the god of the Ancient Wisdom. The caduceus is also a symbol of the Logos, or the creative Word or Fiat, which becomes the universal, fecundating principle of the cosmos. The two intertwined serpents of the caduceus are referred to in the Masonic Teachings.

The serpent encircled rod surmounted with two out-spread wings belongs to the profound symbolism of the number 8 and represents the lemniscate currents of life force which sweep the earth passing through every living form from the body of the earth itself down to its most minute organism. It is the uniting of the two currents, one positive and the other negative, which produces the equilibrium that results in the circulation of force. This force, or Essence of Life and Spirit, impresses its cosmic signature in the form of the figure 8 on every earthly form. In the body of man these currents become radiations of light, flowing out from the sympathetic and the cerebro-spinal nervous systems, when the consciousness is elevated above the material to the spiritual.

Eight is the feminine, the negative, the primeval Mother or Water Principle. In the words of a Masonic writer, "The figure 8 is formed by drawing a line around a woman's breasts, each in turn, thus is symbolized re-creation." This is the true keyword of 8. The ancients describe the eight-faced God with a face toward each of the four points of the compass and also a face toward each of the four intermediate points.

We have stressed the cosmic aspects of 8 in order that we may understand how impossible it is for an 8 soul or destiny path to be narrowly circumscribed in consciousness or environment. The vast spaces are always calling. The inner voice of 8 is ever speaking unutterable things. On the outstretched wings of the Caduceus he must be out and away breathing a rarefied air if he is to do his best work and realize the high idealism of which his soul is ever conscious. He must be free and untrammeled to follow Moses to the heights of Mt Nebo, the peak of Wisdom, there to meet God face to face and to know the glory of a divine transfiguration. Eight in its highest expression elevates man from the realms of mortality to his true position within the radiance of spiritual being.

Sea green is the color of 8, and the Caduceus its symbol. The eighth zodiacal sign, Scorpio, is the emblem of death and also of immortality; it is for the native to choose which of the two it shall be, , the path of the beast or the way of the eagle. The casket is encircled with the rainbow.

The Dragon, or the Serpent, is symbolically related to the number 8. The serpentine or cyclic ebb and flow of all life currents have been shown to be the origin of the cosmic 8. It was the misuse of this serpentine life current within the body of man which caused him to become an exile from the Edenic Garden. When this is understood and the currents corrected through regeneration the gates will open on the New Jerusalem. "That which ascends is the same as that which descends."

A symbolic picture of the New Age depicts a stormy sea typifying the travail of overcoming the turbulence of earthly life. Above the waters shine 8 clear, brilliant stars. A young girl stands with one foot on land, one on sea. In her hands she holds two cups from which flow Charity or Love and Equality or Universal Brotherhood. Above her head shines an eight-pointed star, and near her is an open flower above which is poised a butterfly with wide-stretched wings. This figure represents Truth. The picture as a whole represents symbolically the illumined 8.

Key words of this number are freedom, expansion,

progression, regeneration, and transfiguration.

> "The masses move in cycles. The wise man moves in spirals."

The eighth sephira, or branch of the kaballistic Tree of Life, is the letter H, or Hod in Hebrew, meaning splendor. Such is the condition of the New Order brought forth by the 8 after the cycle of 7 has prepared the way and completed its septenary task. The illumined consciousness of that New Order is described by Paul in the fifteenth chapter of I Corinthians wherein he speaks of the mortal putting on immortality and the corruptible becoming incorruptible.

Eight is the consciousness which, spanning heaven and earth, manifests the powers of conscious Invisible Helpership. At its highest, it gives extended perception and transcendental powers. Not until these are acquired and exercised can the 8 experience true satisfaction of soul.

All secret wisdom is hidden in number, declared the Ageless Wisdom. Eight is the power of that divine darkness, which is no darkness save to outer perception and ignorance. To the inner knowing it is the refracted glory of a light supernal, a light which knows neither shadow or turning. It is the dazzling luminosity in which John, the beloved, visioned the Celestial City.

The 8 offers no half-way measures. It is either personal limitation or spiritual freedom, splendor or degradation, the casket or the rainbow, the terrestrial or the celestial. Eight may grovel in the material, the bestial or soar upon the wings of the Caduceus into immortal spheres, returning as a prophet of glory, a messenger of the joys of an eternal life. The word "sheep" so often used in the Bible contains the spiritual rhythm of 8.

Eight holds the secret to Balance. The power of Polarity is contained within it. Toward its powers, the heart of the world is striving, either consciously or unconsciously. To attain its qualities is the great task before humanity at this time.

Hermes Trismegistus, the thrice-great Egyptian sage, declared many thousands of. years ago that the principle work of the present Fifth Root Race would be the attainment of Balance.

That this is still far from being realized in the mass of humanity is evident in the inharmonious conditions generally prevalent everywhere and which manifest as pain, poverty, disease, and death.

The ancient symbol representing this discordant condition of man is a blindfolded feminine figure holding a pair of scales. The profound wisdom of the ancients is shown in their use of this symbol which so adequately depicts the condition of humanity in this modern day, when the climax of unbalance has been reached. The scales are about to turn. When they do there will be a tremendous, physical, economic, social and religious upheaval, resulting in deep sorrow and suffering. Then the bandage will be withdrawn from the eyes of the figure (mass humanity). God will "wipe away all tears," and the eyes will again see clearly.

The primary note of the celestial rhythms of 8 has been expressed in the following words: "From the field of sin and punishment thou shalt pass into the boundless freedom of my divine protection."

K E Y W O R D

The full orbed cipher represents the Divine Feminine; if broken or imperfect, abasement is denoted; if complete, regeneration and union with spirit is designated.

NOTE: These lessons are not intended for casual reading, but for careful study and meditation wherein it is hoped that by a lifting and acceleration of consciousness, the student may be able to contact more fully the inner man, that source of wisdom and light eternal which makes life complete both within and without.

THE NUMBER NINE

> "Man fell by proceeding from Four to Nine, and
> can only be restored to himself by returning
> from Nine to Four. The passage from Four to
> Nine is the passage from spirit to matter, which
> in dissolution, according to numbers, gives
> Nine."
> — *St. Martin*

Nine is the emblem of matter which, while changing and in
constant flux, yet retains its identity and resists complete
destruction. This is manifest in the strange phenomenon of 9
remaining 9 in its power no matter by what number it is
multiplied. It eternally reproduces itself.

John Heydon, an early Rosicrucian philosopher, writes in
The Holy Guide, published in 1662, that the number 9 if writ
or engraved on silver or sardis, rendered the one who wore it
invisible. He adds further: "Nine also obtaineth the love of
women. It prevails against plagues and fevers. It causeth long life
and health. By this number Plato so ordered events that he died
at the age of 9x9."

Nine has special significance for humanity since it is the
number principally governing its evolution. Around the power of
9 the cyclic progress of man revolves. That 9 is the number of
the evolution of present humanity is borne out by two numbers
in the Book of Revelation, a book which indeed reveals
mysteries. These two numbers are 666 and 144,000. Both
reduce to 9. The former is the number of the Beast, the
unregenerate nature of man that wars against his higher nature,
the mortality that must put on immortality. The latter number,
144,000, is the number of the redeemed. They comprise all who
bear the mark of God upon their foreheads and chant hosannas

in their joy of having found the peace that resides at the heart of their divine Selfhood.

Since all humanity experiences the downward draw of the lower nature and the upward pull of the higher self, it is clear that 666, the Beast, and 144,000, the Regenerated, apply not to a single dragon nor to a specific group of individuals but that they are numerical symbols for powers operating in all humanity, and that both numbers reducing to 9 point to it as the major vibratory power governing human evolution. It makes it clear that this number relates both to the mortal and the immortal, the terrestrial and the celestial aspects of man.

It is because of this inclusive nature of 9 that it becomes the special numerical power by which man comes into contact with his inner self, unfolds his latent divinity, and attains to that state of interior illumination which is known by the name of Initiation.

The esoteric members among the early Christians said that there were 9 orders of angels, by which they meant the 9 celestial Hierarchies that form the evolutionary ladder which extends from God to man. They are so numbered by Dante in *The Divine Comedy*.

The celestial Orders are the 9 which are most intimately concerned with human evolution. Astrologically they correlate to the signs beginning with Cancer and ending with Pisces. Botticelli beautifully portrays these various groups of heavenly Beings in his masterpiece *The Assumption of the Virgin*.

Nine may be represented by the 3 triangles symbolizing the threefold aspects of each of the three principles of man, namely, body, soul, and spirit. This fact also indicates 9 as a number of universality, of a wide, all-embracing consciousness. The 9 individual has run the gamut of personal experiences, including both the high and the low, the mundane and the spiritual. It is the synthesis of these experiences which produces that sympathy, compassion, and a rare understanding which is characteristic of the 9.

Red, the color of humanitarianism, is the color of 9. This means that 9 has a sympathetic understanding of the undeveloped and the underpriviledged while at the same time sharing the aspiration and idealism of the more advanced. Nine is closely related to 10, the number of unity. It is moving toward the consciousness in which all parts are realized as embraced in the One. Nine carries in its heart the red of humanity's sorrow and travail, which, when fully redeemed, will yield to the golden flame of One.

Zodiacally the ninth sign is Sagittarius, the sign of the higher or Christed mind, the place of holy aspiration and inspiration. Nine is the number of universality, cosmic freedom, and high soul expression. Its emblems are a helmet and an olive branch.

That 9 synthesizes the Ego's entire experience gathered throughout the whole of the evolutionary journey prior to its complete reunion with God, or One, is revealed by the numerical truth that all numbers from 1 to 9 reduce to 9. 1 plus 8 equals 9, 2 plus 7 equals 9, 3 plus 6 equals 9, 4 plus 5 equals 9. Thus 9 is truly the number of matter, the number of man's evolution, and the number of cosmic knowing or Initiation.

The numbers 1-2-3-4-5-6-7-8-9-10 equals 9. Also 9-18-27-36-45-54-63-72-81-90 equal 9. Nine when multiplied by another number always reproduces itself; for example, 9 X 2 equals 18, or 9. 9 X 3 equals 27 or 9. 9 X 4 equals 36, or 9. 9 X 10 equals 90, or 9. 1 and 8 are 9, 2 and 7 are 9. 3 and 6 are 9. 4 and 5 are 9. Thus we see how the number 9 returns to itself after the numerous changes through which it may pass by addition, subtraction, or multiplication with other numbers. It indicates at once its power and its universality. The Greeks compared 9 to the ocean, because they said it was like the water flowing around the other numbers, as in the decad. No further elementary number is possible, they added, hence it is like the horizon, because all numbers are bounded by it. Nine is the number of the circumference of things, every circle having 360 degrees, which number digits 9.

Nine is frequently a number of service. A 9 character, therefore, realizes himself fully through service to others. He cannot work successfully for self alone. It must be for the benefit of the whole. The 9 person also has the qualities that make for friendship. He has friends because he is a friend.

A 9 year is especially favorable for cementing old ties and forming new ones. It is also a time that brings favors and gifts from friends. It may be called a veritable friendship year.

Number is the basis of all formation, the root of all creative manifestation. In the number symbolism of a race we may discern its inner response to the forces of life and its understanding of the mysteries of being, both infinite and finite. The fundamentals of geometry and mathematics are cosmic in their origin. The numerals from 1 to 10 compose the sound and power hieroglyph by which the worlds are made. They are centers of condensed creative potency in materialization.

The similarity of these glyphs as used by different races, even primitive peoples, indicate that there is present in the number itself a hidden power that expresses itself in its every symbol though that power may not be consciously recognized by those who design the symbols.

Every system utilizes a circle enclosing a point, a triangle, and a cube. These are followed in some form by the pentagram, the hexad, the heptad, the octad, the ennead, and the decad. In these cosmic hieroglyphics from 1 to 10 may be found the astral delineations of the Book of Genesis; the separation of the grosser substances from the finer, or the formations which constituted the work of the Seven Creative Days. Also herein may be traced the creation of man and his loss of the Edenic state, and the path of emancipation which leads to the eventual reunion with his real or higher self.

Nine marks the beginning of this reunion. Its symbol, made

of the line and the circle, represent the masculine and feminine principles potentially united and in active and conscious simultaneous manifestation. But equilibrium is not fully attained in 9; perfect balance is not yet realized. Because of this fact 9 has been considered to be both a favorable and unfavorable number. It has been termed the number of evil and also described as representing the Tree of Eternal Life in the Garden of the Gods.

Thus we see from its wide and varied influences that the 9 may make what he will of life. All things are fundamentally and intrinsically good, evil being but good in the becoming. Man through his own God-given power within himself, possess the ability to rise superior to any outward circumstances and to overcome and master any malign influence. He may yield to failure or he may rise to the glorious heights of Initiation. Nine is the number of the Initiate.

The Temple in which Pythagoras taught was dedicated to "The Nine." These were the 9 Muses of Grecian mythology, the daughters of Zeus and the goddess of memory. Their names and the department of life to which they gave their inspiration were as follows:

Calliope	. . . . Poetry	Erato	. . . . Love
Cleo	. . . . . .History	Terpsichore	. . Dancing
Melpomene	. . Tragedy	Urania	. . .Astronomy
Euterpe	. . . . .Music	Thalia	. . . . Comedy
Polyhymnia	. . . . Eliquence		

These 9 muses represent the many faculties and attributes acquired by the aspirant as he passes through the 9 degrees of the Mysteries. Rhythms of mind and body were developed as acquisitions of an expanding consciousness in a measure of perfection and beauty entirely unrecognized or unsuspected by the majority in our present materialistic civilization.

That the Greeks were masters of the arts and reached a degree of excellence in symmetry, proportion, and grce which has never been equaled by any succeeding generations was due to the Arcane Wisdom given them in the Mystery Temples of that day. This modern age must return to like shrines of hidden truth and do homage before them before it can attain to that same high degree of aesthetic excellence attained by the Greeks. The 9 may become a prominent exponent of this truth and a leader among those who have the courage to blaze the trail which will guide the less dauntless ones to find again the paths which pass into these Temples of Light.

Nine is the figure 6 (a symbol of sex) reversed. Nine in its highest aspect, therefore, represents the sublimation of the creative life essences which is the fundamental teaching of Initiation. The story of the Widow's Son of Naim as recorded in the Luke's gospel is that of such an Illumination. The word Naim means 9 and refers to one who has passed successfully through the 9 steps of Enlightenment which lifts the consciousness of man above and beyond the ken of ordinary humanity. Virgil's famous Epic, *The Aeneid* (the Nine), is an occult cypher which also records the experiences of this same inner growth and development.

Among the biblical characters and Sacred Books which are attuned to the vibratory rhythms of 9 are some of the most deeply mystical in the entire category of the Book of Books. One of these is The Song of Solomon which is a chant of the mystic marriage and which voices the ecstasy of a soul that has glimpsed the heights of cosmic freedom and returned to sing of the glory of that liberation which none who still remain in bondage to the things of earth can ever know. This is the glorious freedom of 9 when it has become a soul number.

Another Book which is keyed to the inner power of 9 is that enigmatic story of Job. When this is spiritually interpreted, it is found to be an account of a soul who wins emancipation by learning to rise above the limitations of human travail and personal bondage. It delineates the cosmic pattern of 9 by which that freedom is attained.

The mysterious Book of Daniel is also in tune with 9. Daniel, the prophetic Seer who visioned the occurrences of past ages and linked them through his initiatory knowledge with happenings yet to be, was, like the Pythagoreans, dedicated to the cosmic wisdom of "The Nine."

Agrippa writes of the Philosopher's Stone that "it is blood-red like fire and white and transparent like heaven." These are the colors of Nine. "It is," he adds, "composed of One and Three and at the same time, of Four and Five."

Five represents man, the microcosm; also the 5 senses. It is the number of the Root Races which, up to this time have embodied the spirit during its evolutionary cycles. Four represents the square of matter formed by the condensation of the 4 elements; also the 4 Sacred Seasons in which man may learn to transform matter into spirit and thus ascend from his present human status into one of a higher order. This theme sounds the central keynote of the Book of Job.

The Tabernacle (Mystery Temple) in the Wilderness, presided over by the Initiate Moses, symbolized the hidden power of 4 and 5, or 9, by five pillars of shittim wood from which were suspended four-colored curtains. These curtains concealed the inner place from the outer, and could be lifted only by one who had earned the privilege to pass within the holy precinct. The illumined 9 becomes worthy of this priceless privilege. In the words of a prophet such a one is portrayed as "a winged creature yet bearing the likeness of a man," or as Paul describes him, "an heir and a joint heir with Christ." This is the supreme ideal and the destiny of every soul keyed to the celestial note of 9.

The ninth letter of the sacred Hebrew alphabet is Teth, meaning "Serpent." The word serpent is closely associated in our mind with the Garden of Eden and the Genesis legend of the expulsion of Adam and Eve therefrom on account of the subtle wiles of this crawling beast. Some variation of this story is common to all the principal religions of the world.

One of the most magnificent episodes in all biblical history is the miracle performed by Moses, the master artificer in white magic, when he transformed the crawling serpents in the dust whose sting brought death into brazen, upright serpents, which when elevated and looked up to by the afflicted brought healing and life. The above serves to indicate inner links between 9, Teth, and serpent, and to bring out another aspect of the number.

Numbers are centers of enormous force and power, each one being a particular focus for specific emanations of the Elohim in their evolutionary work with humanity. "Number," asserts a sage, "veileth the power of the Elohim."

Nine represents the power of sex. In this aspect we recognize the truth of the dual nature of 9 as previously defined, namely, a number of matter and a number of divine illumination. For this the great motive power of all life leads man either into degeneration as instanced in the expulsion of man and woman from the Edenic state of consciousness or else into the paths of regeneration and Initiation as exemplified in John the Revelator's glorious vision of the Woman clothed with the Sun.

It is significant to note that the word "oil" around which is concealed so much biblical mysticism is a 9-powered word. "Wine" is six-powered, and "bread" three-powered. Each of these numbers are a component part of the number 9, and the words mentioned are used throughout the Bible in reference to the various regenerative processes which take place within man as he treads the ninefold path of conscious spiritual expansion known to the early Christians as "The Way." This Way was taught by Moses when he lifted the brazen serpent which healed the ills of all the people.

Love is also a word which is set to the rhythmic harmony of 9. Man will never come into a full realization of the operations of *love* as a *power*, until he walks the "Way," which is the only path to regeneration and redemption. — Nine is the power of the Serpent Wisdom. High and holy is its meaning, and sacred is the responsibility that comes with it. The illumined 9 comes into physical incarnation to serve. For him life is not a playground, but a preparatory school for the higher spiritual grades which his illumined consciousness has glimpsed and into which his soul ardor may lift him.

The ninth Sephira is Yesod, termed "the Foundation." — The Tarot symbol for 9 is a hermit in a mantle, leaning upon a staff and carrying a half-concealed lamp. When the light becomes full it reveals the mantle as the seamless robe of the master. "Count aright and then thou shalt have oil for thy lamps," sing the Wise Men of all times. — The functions of 9 are described by Paul Case in the *Book of Tokens* as follows:

> "This is the Serpent of Temptation,
> Yet from it cometh forth redemption.
> For the Serpent is the first appearance of the
>   of the Anointed One,
> And that which casteth Adam out from
>   the Garden of the East,
> Even that shall bring him back once more
>   to Paradise."

The Christ gave this same truth when He said: "If I be lifted up I will draw all others unto me."

KEY THOUGHTS

"Nine which is three-Squared, refers to the attianment of perfection on three lower planes." — "Abraham had reached the period of ninety and nine years when he communed with angels and his name became no longer Abram but Abraham."

THE NUMBER TEN

> The number 10 is an all-embracing number;
> outside of it none other exists, for what is
> beyond 10 returns again to units.   — *Kabbalah*

> When the Concealed of the Concealed wanted
> to reveal Himself, He first made a point which
> shaped into a sacred form and covered it with a
> rich and splendid garment which is the world.
>
> — *The Zohar*

The above quotation from the Zohar well describes the productive element which is embodied in the number 10, the number that completes all numbers.

Ten is formed of the pillar and the circle (10), the masculine and feminine, or the Father-Mother God principles respectively, by which all things are created. It represents the productive powers active in the Garden of Eden and which were expressed by Adam (man) and Eve (woman) before whom all created things were brought and by whom they were named. The words male and female digit 10.

The names assigned to created things bear a profound occult significance in relation to numbers. Every name vibrates to a certain number. That number is, therefore, the very soul of the name. Herein lies the secret power of the spoken word, for when the syllables of a name are sounded, the corresponding powers of its number are released and may be used by one who has the wisdom to manipulate this subtle force. In this connection, meditate on thy promise: "Whatsoever ye ask in my name, shall be done unto you."

Modern man has much to learn from the ancients in regard

to the power of the spoken word. "Words are spirit and they are life," said Christ Jesus.

It was also the Master who declared: "By thy words thou shalt be justified, and by thy words thou shalt be condemned." How much more this means than current orthodox interpretations ascribe to it! Words possess tone, color and form. They are active powers for good or ill. Speech therefore, is a sacred creative thing.

Words keyed to the rhythm of 10 are creative in a special sense; they are productive; they have the power of attraction or acquisition. These qualities characterize a 10 person. Such an individual is a center of force whose influence is wide and pronounced. He respondes decisively to whatever karmic reactions he experiences in life. It may be for either good or ill depending on whether he uses his powers wisely in accordance with the dictates of the spirit or if he yields to personal inclinations regardless of the promptings of the Higher Self. But on whatever plane a 10 expresses himself, he is a person of power.

Ten is the number from which all things have come and into which all must return. It represents both the divine Outbreathing (masculine) and Inbreathing (feminine); it is the power of the dual process of involution and evolution.

Unconditioned unity may be ascribed to the First Great Cause. Oneness of Being preceded differentiated manifestation. As differentiation proceeded, 10 principles became active. These are represented biblically by 10 of Jacob's 12 sons.

Numbers are the divine hieroglyphics of the Supreme Being. Inharmonious relationships in the body and life of man, and in nature around us, are a direct result of the wrong or negative application of one or more of these principles. All numbers beyond 10 are but different combinations of the fundamental 10.

Pythagoras called 10 the tetrachtys and so arranged it.

This figure is formed of the Hebrew letter yod, the tenth in the alphabet of 22, and is considered the most occult of all the Hebrew letters. The Kabbalah refers to the letter yod as the Workman of Deity.

Yod correlates to the tenth sign of the zodiac, Capricorn. Among the ancients this sign was represented by the Makara or great beast, and in later times a creature half goat and half fish. A person attuned to ten is like one coming under the sign Capricorn in that he does not know his latent capabilities until he is spiritually awakened. Incidentally, the constellation Capricorn numbers 29 stars, thus coming under the numerical emanation of 10.

Pythagoras illustrates the influence of 10 by the following allegory: "A man was seen bent and aged from the burden of his load. On being asked of what it was constituted, he declared it was the letter yod.

Yod embodies both the masculine and feminine potencies and the symbol is incorporated in some form in each of the 22 letters of the Hebrew alphabet.

If there be a single word by which the nature and the quality of yod can best be described, that word is *life*.

Ten is the fundamental and formative number of the Old Testament. The patriarchs from Adam to Noah are 10 in number. The cosmic principles given to Moses in the forty-day vision on the Mount when he stood face to face with God as with a friend, and which constitute the basis of the present Aryan civilization, were set to the rhythms of 10. This was in conformity with the masculine-feminine composition of the race which in its dual aspect comes under the dual-symboled figure

10 as previously noted.

St. Martin gives us the following mystical interpretations of the decad:

> By the union of the spiritual septenary to the temporal ternary we have the famous denary ever present to our thoughts. As the image of the Divinity Itself, It accomplishes the reconciliation of all beings by causing them to return into unity. The temperal denary is composed of two numbers, 7 and 3; but its type connects with unity and is not subject to any division.

> So long as numbers are united with the decad, none of them present the image of deformity or corruption, these characteristics manifesting only the separation period. Among the numbers thus specialized, some are absolutely sad, such as 2 and 5, which alone divide the denary. Others suffer in active operation, as 3, 6, and 9. Nothing of this is seen in the complete decad, for in that supreme order there is no deformity, illusion or suffering.

Ten intones the powers of the unmanifested Universe whence all things proceed. Seven inscribes the forces of the universe in manifestation. This creation or appearance is brought about through the threefold operation of the Trinity, the 3 in 1. The Supreme Being responds to the completion of the decad; the God of the Solar System to the harmony of the ternary; and the planetary Spirits to the building powers of the septenary. This at least suggests the 10 or unity, which is the Tonic in the cosmic chord; the three-powered Godhead intones the ternary which becomes the Dominant; and the planetary Gods are the building forces of the septenary in their processes of creation which becomes the Sub-Dominant in the celestial music.

Ten is the pure white light of One. It synthesizes all the colors of the spectrum. It blends and harmonizes the tones of all the 7 planes of being into a single rhythmic unity. The

Kabbalistic symbol of 10 is the Tree of Life with its 10 gleaming sephireth or centers of life and power.

The advanced individual who has 10 as his destiny number fulfills his life most fruitfully by coordinating and interpreting the manifold movements and aspirations making for peace, fellowship and amity among the nations and races of the world. He speaks the universal language that brings the divergent peoples of the earth into a harmonious human unit. His word is power and his presence peace.

In discussing the numerical path of unity, Agrippa observes that "By passing the number seven into the number ten there may be a progress to the supreme unity upon which all virtue and wonderful operations depend."

The Kabbalah refers to this same power of Cosmic Numerology in the legend of the Ten Wise Men who enter the secret mystery chambers of the Yod, 7 of whom return to their work in the outer world, and 3 of whom remain to operate in secrecy and invisibility.

Genesis 18:28-33

Peradventure there shall lack five of the fifty righteous; wilt thou destroy all the city for lack of five? And he said, If I find there forty and five, I will not destroy it.

And he spake unto him yet again, and said, Peradventure there shall be forty found there. And he said, I will not do it for the forty's sake.

And he said unto him, Oh let not the Lord be angry, and I will speak: Peradventure there shall thirty be found there. And he said, I will not do it, if I find thirty there.

And he said, Behold now, I have taken upon me to speak unto the Lord: Peradventure there shall be twenty found there. And he said, I will not destroy it for twenty's sake.

And he said, Oh let not the Lord be angry, and I will
speak yet but this once: Peradventure ten shall be found
there. And he said. I will not destroy it for ten's sake.

And the Lord went his way, as soon as he had left
communing with Abraham; and Abraham returned unto
his place.

Abraham did not go below the number 10 in his effort to
save Sodom and Gomorrah. In 10 wholeness or salvation was
possible. In 10 the masculine (1) and the feminine (0) stand
together in equality. It was not so in Sodom and Gomorrah. The
feminine or love principle had been desecrated. It is the fall of
the emotional nature that is symbolized by the fiery destruction
of the two wicked cities. If 10, the power of the feminine in
regeneration, could have been uplifted and brought into
equilibrium with the masculine or will principle, the cause for
the destruction of the cities would have been removed and its
inhabitants saved.

Gomorrah is a nine-powered name; Sodom is three-powered.
These values indicate the path of redemption and a return to
unity.

Israel is a three-powered word; its forces become the
keynote of Jacob's life after he had wrestled with the angel.

Genesis 32:27-28

And he said unto him, What is thy name? And he said
Jacob. And he said, Thy name shall no more be called
Jacob, but Israel: for as a prince hast thou power with
God and with men, and hast prevailed.

The syllable 'is' is feminine and comes from the name of the
Egyptian goddess Isis; 'ra' is masculine and is the name of the
Egyptian sun god; 'el' joins the two into a harmonious unity
which no external conditions can ever disturb. Such a one is

Israel.

Such is the ideal attainment for the 10 individual. His key word was given by the angel to Jacob: "Thou hast power with God and with men, and hast prevailed."

The First and Second Books of Chronicles are keyed to 10. They are chronicles of the spirit in search of its own inner completion and unity. They begin with the line of Noah, representative of the Fifth Root Race peoples and outline their history up to the time of the destruction of Jerusalem, which marked the failure of humanity in general to attain to the high state of consciousness which had been set before it as a possibility.

The way of this high attainment has been open always for the few. This is indicated in Chronicles in the account of the visit of the Queen of Sheba to Solomon, the wisdom king. The Books of Chronicles point the way of the 10 as the masses know it. This is the way of struggle and conflict, inharmony and unbalance between man and woman. It is the way that leads to the destruction of Jerusalem. The Books also reveal the secret way of 10, the veritable highway of the king, which leads to harmony, balance, unity and completion within the individual himself. This is the state that will ultimately culminate in that inner peace that passeth understanding, and outwardly in the restoration of Jerusalem, the city of peace. The way is indicated by which the spirit will be restored to its original state of completeness within.

The growth and the development of the cosmos, and man's relation thereto, are revealed in the esoteric study of numbers. It is for this reason the masonic candidate is admonished to study mathematics and the science of the stars.

As previously stated, the numbers 3, 7 and 10 compose the corner stone of our planetary cosmogony. Concerning the 10 in this connection Hermes writes:

> Ten is the mother of the Soul, for life and light are

therein united. For the number one is born from Spirit
and the number ten from matter (chaos, feminine); the
Unity has made the ten and the ten the Unity.

The word decad means esoterically, that all has been
accomplished. Ten reaches the supreme heights in numbers; in
order to exceed 10 we must begin another series by returning to
the monad.

The kabbalistic Tree is formed of the Ten Sephiroth, or
points of Light, through which the entire process of creation is
given numerically.

One is God, and in the Zohar, or Book of Light, is described
thus:

The Infinite was entirely unknown and diffused no light
i42,   before the luminous point broke through into vision.

Nine is man. Nine and 1 together reveal God in man. Five is
man apart from God in individualization. Nine is man returned
to God. When this is understood and accomplished, the work of
10 is undertaken.

Ten is the recipient of all numbers; and hence, in the words
of a writer on the subject, "It is the recipient of all heaven
which was ordained to receive all men; also eternity, which is
infinite life; because it contains every number within itself, and
number is infinite."

The most ancient and at the same time the most complete
of all symbols given by the Wise Ones for the edification of man
is the circle with a dot in its center. An elongation of the
central dot gives the symbol of the number 10. This symbol
represents totality, completeness; it is the *sumum bonum* of all
creation; it is God in manifestation through His manifold
creations.

As previously stated, numbers are focii of great spiritual
power emanating from the Elohim who are guarding the destiny
of earth.

The number with which man is most closely attuned is the one which holds the conditions and powers through which the soul learns its chief lesson in a particular incarnation. Each spirit inherently is made in the image and likeness of God, and even though this truth is shut away from him by veils of intense materialism, the experiences of each life cycle are destined to bring him nearer to the time when his soul will be bared to the glorious revelation of his innate divinity. It is the unfoldment of this latent godhood that constitutes the supreme purpose and goal of existence. To know God, or all good, is the goal of all mankind.

This consummation is represented by the number 10. Thus this number has been rightly termed the end of the Divine Series, "the image of potential manifestation and of spiritual duration."

Yod, the tenth letter of the Hebrew alphabet, denotes spiritual perfection. This significance of 10 suggests the statement of the Ancient Wisdom that the "Ten made manifest are also Seven, and these are the Elohim. These Seven bring forth ten again."

One of the most significant biblical words which carries the emanations of 10 is the word 'stone'. A study of its repeated use in biblical lore will give additional understanding as to the inner meaning and power of 10.

In Matthew 16:18 we read: "Thou art Peter, and upon this rock I will build my church." The name Peter is from the Greek word 'Petros', meaning rock, and the word stone is frequently used in the Bible in a sense similar to that above. It is a twice 10-powered word, its numerical value being 20.

The following lines from the Book of Tokens by Paul Case are to be found in this connection:

　　I am Ten,
　　Yet in me proceedeth the twenty,
　　For I am Ten Ineffable,

And Ten manifested in Creation,
Therefore is Yod both Ten and Twenty.

In the Book of Revelation we learn that those who have made themselves worthy to know the Christ at His second coming are those who have the tenfold power written upon their foreheads. (Rev. 2:17, 22:4).

The Tarot symbol depicting the power of 10 is the wheel of fortune surmounted by a sphinx with a drawn sword ready to cut the threads of fate whenever the signal is given by the four Recording Angels who stand on guard about the wheel.

These Angels are the four Elohim pictorially represented by a lion, an eagle, an ox and a man. Leo and Scorpio are five-powered words (half of 10). Taurus is a 10 word and Aquarius an 8. The keynote of 8 is Polarity which is the keyword of the New Aquarian Age. The 10 plagues of Bible history symbolize earth experiences that lead to the high spiritual revealings of 10. They represent the various impacts of the Wheel of Fortune during the cycle of earth lives by which we are aroused to action and attainment. A 10 individual is always an old soul, one who has known many lives of both high and low degree and who has learned how transitory are things of earth alone.

The tenth Sephira is Malkuth, the foundation, or the Virgin Kingdom. It is man-woman, head-heart, spirit-soul, united and redeemed. "One (1) is my inmost being; 2 is my self-utterance."

KEY THOUGHTS: "The Ten signifies purification; for to the number Seven which embraces all created things, is added the Trinity of Creation."

In the Book of Genesis we read: "The waters decreased continually until the tenth month; on the first day of that month were the tops of the mountains seen."

THE NUMBER ELEVEN

He gave to each a number and a name which
only he knew who received it.
                                    —*Revelation 11:17.*

"Having permeated this whole universe with
one fragment of myself, I remain."

Eleven and twenty-two are master numbers. Unlike every
other number composed of two or more digits, they are never
reduced to a single numeral but remain as they are, unchanged.
Words and names bearing the vibratory values of either of these
numbers have in them powers that make for attainment,
supremacy and mastership.

Among words of power in the several kingdoms of nature
that vibrate to these numbers may be noted iron, one of the
foremost of metals for strength and utility. Its number is 11. In
the plant kingdom the lily is 22. The horse, a pioneer among
animals, is an 11. The highest product of earth's humanity is the
Master Jesus, whose name carries the power of attainment and
self-mastery which operates through 11. By angelic instruction
He was so named. Later, at the time of baptism into the mystic
waters of Jordan, He demonstrated His human mastery by
becoming a vehicle of the Christ, a Being of a higher order of
life and the Saviour of the world.

The name Christ vibrates to 5. It indicates the awakening of
inner powers of individualization. Under its influence the divine
spirit within becomes manifest. The name Christ Jesus (5, 11)
vibrates to 7, the earth's planetary number, thus harmonizing
with the fact that Jesus became the Christed man or the Cosmic

93

Pattern for the inspiration and emulation of the entire human race.

The doctrine of the Trinity in one form or another, is fundamental to all religions. In the Christian religion the threefold Godhead is composed of the Father, Son, and Holy Ghost. This triune Principle contains the power of 1, 2, and 3, which together form the working basis of the triple activity by which all creation proceeds. "When One wills to create, One becomes many, all threefold".

One, two and three constitute the forces of Will, Wisdom and Activity, which underly all manifestation. They are the forces which build the outer or form world, including the bodies of man. All things on earth are moulded in conformity with an astral or starry pattern. It is this celestial formation of man which was "made in the image and likeness of God".

The purpose of earth evolution is to develop man into a creator, working in harmony with the divine plan. The lessons necessary to that development come through the vibratory rhythms of number. As man reaches the higher stages, he responds to the master forces of 9, 11 and 22. Eleven amplifies the powers of 1; 22 does the same for the forces of 2; and 9 acts in a like relation to 3.

When these forces become fully active in man, he acquires the ability to create new conditions, a new body, and a new life, all in harmony with the divine image in whose likeness he was fasioned in the Beginning. This state of attainment was referred to as the birth of the Christ within.

From what has been said, it becomes apparent that 9, 11 and 22 constitute a higher trinity of power than do 1, 2 and 3. That higher trinity holds the potencies by which humanity will ultimately realize its highest ideals. Incidentally, it may be noted that the added numerals of both trinities reduce to 6, a number under which latent powers are unfolded.

The numbers 11 and 22 vibrate to all the 7 tones of the

musical scale. They also respond to the entire planetary octave. By their inclusive powers the Christ consciousness will be brought ultimately to perfect fruition into the life of mankind.

In the mystic series of initiatory signposts, the Hebrew alphabet, the eleventh of its 22 letters if Kaph, which is represented by a maiden closing the mouth of a Lion. Astrologically interpreted, the maiden is Virgo, the Lion, Leo. (The 5th and 6th signs equals 11). Spiritually, Virgo correlates to the feminine principle; Leo the masculine. On the physical plane the masculine dominates the feminine but in the alchemical processes of regeneration, the feminine overcomes this disability. The feminine pole of the spirit is then brought into perfect balance with the masculine. In terms of masonic symbolism, the fallen column of the two which stand at the entrance to the Temple is restored to its upright position. Equilibrium, the soul name for 11, is accomplished.

The cross has been used extensively in sacred symbology both before and after its adoption as the emblem of Christian religion. One of its arms is upright, the other horizontal. This is another representation of the fallen pole, the feminine or Eve principle in man. When this principle will be lifted and brought into perfect balance with the masculine, the cross of struggle, sorrow and sacrifice will yield as a symbol of man's religious aspirations to the two upright columns (11) as the symbol of attainment. It will mark the redemption of the fallen, the cessation of strife, and the realization of at-one-ment with the divine.

The Christ manifested the body that is built under the powers of 11. In the mystic interval between the Resurrection and the Ascension when He gave His deepest teachings to those closest to Him, He appeared to His Disciples, bidding them to view Him in His garment of light. "Behold my hands and feet", said He, "that it is myself; handle me, and see, for a spirit hath not flesh and bones as ye see me have".

The Christ here described the regenerated body which is immune to disease, age, and even death itself. This immortal vehicle which He built for Himself, He taught all others how to build, for He came as the Life, the Way, and the Truth. All who follow His precepts and in His steps may do the works that He did, and by His own premise, even greater.

The powers of 11 are symbolically referred to in the passage quoted above. The hands represent the masculine principles of Fire and Air; the feet, the feminine principles of Water and Earth. When these four principles are perfectly blended the equilibrium of 11 is attained.

Masons are taught that 11 is the most important number, because "with the possession *within* of two Units (equilibrium) one may come into possession of all things". This being true, 11 becomes the priestly messenger bringing to all mankind the "glad tidings of great joy".

The Ancient Wisdom defines the powers of 11 as follows: "In my grasp are all things held in perfect equilibrium; I bind all opposites together, each to its complement".

These words describe accurately the powers of 11. Ages will pass before they will be fully understood by the majority, and yet more ages before they will become generally manifest in the life of the many. The same is true of 22. These two numbers, 11 and 22, are secret workers — silent, aloof, and alone; their workshop is the cosmos, and their tools are latent forces of the divinity residing in the heart of all life.

Jesus, as previously noted, working directly with the powers of 11, made equilibrium the keynote of his ministry. Joshua, another form of the name Jesus, also attained to the state of Balance. This is indicated astrologically in his ability to make the sun and the moon stand still in the heavens numerologically, in his age which was 11 years.

When 1 becomes 11 the individual interests are merged into the universal and the fire of passion is transmuted into the light of compassion. The qualities of brotherhood and universality become manifest in such a one, and their extension into the consciousness of the race the chief objective of life. The illumined 11 is, figuratively speaking, a pilgrim and a wanderer, with no abiding place except in the minds and hearts of those who need him. Such can truly say with Thomas Paine that "the world is my home and to do good my religion".

Eleven embraces the opposites in both heaven and hell. Both vibrate to 11, and Jesus, an 11, lived, and loved, and served in both.

The two upright columns before the entrance of every Mystery Temple, the Masonic included, are synonyms of the power and purpose of 11. The colors of 11 are black and white, signifying truth latent and active, hidden and revealed. Violet also belongs to 11 and signifies the illumination which the spirit gains through sorrow.

The Books of the Prophets in the Old Testament number 22. This is also the number of Epistles, the Revelation of John included, in the New Testament. While 22, as previously stated, always retains its integrity as it stands, never being reduced to 4, yet it contains the inner vibratory rhythms of the sacred quarternary, as pythagoras called it, and which he refers to in his Golden Verses as a most holy power.

It is the numerical power sounding the keynote of the New Testament Dispensation, the Four Gospels containing the initiatory formulae of the Path which leads to Liberation by the way of the Cross.

In the Hebrew alphabet, Tau, the cross, is the twenty-second letter. It is the final letter in the series of 22. Each letter represents a certain degree of inner illumination. As the powers they hold are developed, they lead to the awakening of the Christ within. The series terminates with the cross (Tau), not as a symbol of pain and tragedy and defeat, but as an emblem of victory over limitation and the release of the spirit into new spheres of freedom. When the Supreme Way-Shower carried the cross up Calvary He was still in the consciousness that had uttered the words, "My yoke is easy and my burden is *Light*".

The cross is universally used as a symbol for the spirit when encased in a physical body. That being its real significance it enters prominently into the symbolism of other religions beside the Christian, and also into the rituals of the Temple Mysteries. To win freedom from the cross is to secure a release from the bondage of matter.

In biblical literature the Book of Numbers is keyed to the number 11. This Book has been compared to the great epics, the Iliad and the Aeneid. While it is only a fragment of an older and more extended treatise on the meaning of numbers, it still contains a treasury of esoteric values.

The Book deals largely with the Israelites' second year's journey in the wilderness. And the "Lord spake unto Moses in the wilderness of Sinai. . . . . on the first day of the *second* month, in the *second* year after they were come out of the land of Egypt".

> Take ye the sum of all the congregation of the children of Israel, after their families, by the house of their fathers, with the number of their names, every man by their polls; from twenty years old and upward, all that are able to go forth to war in Israel: thou and Aaron shall number them by their armies. And with you there shall be a man of every tribe; every one head of the house of his fathers.   – *Numbers 1:2-4*

> And the Lord spake unto Moses, saying, Make thee two trumpets of silver; of a whole piece shalt thou make them: that thou mayst use them for the calling of the assembly, and for the journeying of the camps.
>   – *Numbers 10:12*

The spiritual significance of numbers in relation to the life and works of man appear throughout the entire Bible. It is quite obvious in the numbering of the Tribes of Israel. Each of the twelve received a number, and the specific service assigned to it was in harmony with the number power through and with which it worked. The tribes were also formed into certain assemblages. Each family was also given a number and assigned to a particular place and mission. This was done not merely to facilitate regimentation; it was done primarily as an aid in the fulfillment of the spiritual task they were called to perform. It is also to be remembered that the history of the Israelites is the history of man and every incident connected with them has relation to the spiritual development of the individual. The inheritance of the sons and daughters of Israel is the spiritual heritage of the illumined 11.

The Twelve Tribes correlate to the Twelve Signs of the Zodiac. Each tribe expresses the qualities of a certain sign, just as it manifests the powers of a certain number. These Twelve Signs and their corresponding numbers, are all operative in the life of every individual. Man is himself a universe in miniature. With this in mind. valuable personal application can be made of detailed historical facts contained in the Bible that would otherwise be passed by as having neither interest nor value.

The Book of Ruth is attuned to the rhythm of 22. Esoterically, this beautiful Book contains an account of the mystic marriage whrein the transmuted lower nature is brought into union with the higher. The hitherto divided nature becomes unified. This is the true significance of the number 22. It is because the two are in balanced unity that the 2 Twos remain unchanged. The Book of Ruth is a spiritual textbook for the twenty-two.

Looking first to the characters of the Book of Ruth, we meet Boaz, whose name means "swiftness", or "fleetness of spirit"; Ruth means "faithfulness", the most important qualification of the neophyte. Naomi typifies the forces of cosmic or spiritual law. Her name means "pleasantness". Mara,

99

another name for Naomi, means "bitterness". Thus the two names indicate the pleasantness or bitterness experienced as a result of obedience to or violation of the law of the spirit. The reactions experienced by Orpha, one of the daughters of Naomi, was bitter, since she lived in terms of the personality which she represents, whereas Ruth met with "pleasantness" through faithfulness to the spirit which she symbolized.

Ruth is chosen because of her faithfulness and loyalty to become a gleaner in the corn-fields. Later, after having been further tested as to worthiness and ability by both Naomi and Boaz, she is given a present by Boaz when she meets him at midnight beside a *heap of corn*. There he instructs her in the holy rites of the mystic union which is soon to be consummated, and give to her six measures of barley.

Ruth pledges herself to high and holy living, and follows Naomi into the sacred city of Bethlehem. They arrive just in time for barley harvest. The symbolism is important. Much is concealed in the terms "corn" and "barley". They relate to the high experiences with which the legend deals. The same symbolism was used in the Mysteries of Egypt and Greece which centered in "a reaped cornstock and a mystic marriage". Greek mythology also tells of Persephone returning each year from the underworld through the young corn.

The Book of Ruth closes with the marriage of Ruth and Boaz. The personality has been surmounted and spirit blends with spirit. Their marriage was witnessed by the ten Elders — the powers of 10 through which the masculine and feminine principles come into balance. Under the powers of 11 they attain to perfect equilibrium, and under the master number 22 the mystic wedding is consummated.

The powers of 22 soar above those of 2 as spirit rises above matter. They belong to different octaves of force. By the powers of 22, an amalgamation is effected of the principles of Fire, Air, Water and Earth — and astrologically, of the forces operating through the four fixed signs, Leo, Aquarius, Scorpio and Taurus, which are related to the four principles in the order named. Twenty-two brings the Great Work to completion; the cross becomes the crown.

The early Alchemists described the attainment of 22 as follows: "In every individual of every species there are four elements comprising two males and two females, — by a proper union of these we get a dual being, a second marriage, a new individual".

The "two males and two females" have reference to the four elements of Air, Fire, Earth, Water. When we understand that these also represent the mentality, passions, emotions and the physical body, we recognize wherein the Great Work must always be accomplished.

Twenty-two synthesizes and expands the powers of 11. Eleven develops soul power through loving, selfless service. Twenty-two releases these soul forces. One in whom this occurs becomes a "walker of the skies". He has earned the "Master's wages" and is able to "travel in foreign countries".

Twenty-two is one of power and accomplishment; its colors are cream and coral; its symbol, a cross; and its supreme keyword is LIGHT.

KEY THOUGHTS

Wisdom is the principal thing — therefore get Wisdom: and with all thy getting, get understanding. (Pro. 4:7)

The acquiring of a perfect Balance between two extremes is the supreme purpose of God in creation and of the god in man.

QUESTIONS ON LESSON 11

1. What stage of development is portrayed by the numbers 11 and 22?
2. What correlation is there between 11 and the eleventh zodiacal sign Aquarius?
3. What biblical character can you mention who is attuned to 11?
4. Give keywords particularly descriptive of 11 and 22.

NOTE: These lessons are not intended for casual reading, but for careful study and meditation, wherein it is hoped that by a lifting and acceleration of consciousness, the student may be able to contact more fully the inner man — that source of wisdom and light eternal which makes life complete both within and without.

THE NUMBERS TWELVE AND THIRTEEN

"Each of the Holy Four must be of Himself
threefold."   —*Pythagoras*

In the number 12, the forces of 1 and 2 combine and form
3. In studying the value of 12, the student is advised, therefore,
to review carefully the lessons covering the numbers 1, 2, and 3,
and to meditate upon the sublime powers which their forces
produce in 12. In the number 11 this product is foreshadowed
as an ideal; in 12 it reaches perfect manifestation.

The powers of 12 may be applied to all concepts which deal
with extension, expansion, and elevation. It transcends the three
dimensional. The consciousness belonging to it is posited in a
higher dimension.

In the numbers, 1, 2, and 3 we may trace the gradual
involution of spirit into matter; in the number 12 we may
discover this same working toward its liberation from the
limitations of form. It leads upward and inward. Spiritual forces
gain the ascendancy, and the spirit regains freedom. It wins
liberation from the cross of matter and is resurrected in a
vehicle of light. Time gives way to the timeless, and mortality
enters into conscious immortality. Since this is the nature of 12
it is evident that the full realization of its powers come only
with the expansion and illumination of consciousness belonging
to Initiation.

The twelfth letter of the Hebrew alphabet is Lamed. In
Tarot symbolism this is represented by a man suspended from
his left leg on a gibbet placed between two trees, each tree
having six branches, making 12 in all. These branches have been
cut away, indicating the series of earth experiences put forth

and completed in the long cycle of spiritual unfoldment. No Ego can ever come under the highly differentiated vibratory forces of 12 that has not accumulated an unusual inner strength through many and varied experiences. The 12 vibration belongs to the "old soul."

A person who has attained to the powers of 12 has learned many lessons under the masculine forces of one and passed through many experiences within the feminine rhythm of 2. Twelve also blends the powers of 3 and 9. It is the Holy Trinity in Manifestation. Three works towards the self-mastery which is essential to taking certain degrees of Initiation attainable under 9. Nine is man in generation; 12 is man in regeneration. The supreme purpose of the spirit's pilgrimage through earth experience is to bring to birth the Christ within. The number 12 sounds the keynote of this accomplishment.

Twelve lines of equal length describe the cube. The Mason is taught in the early stages of his exercises that the object of his training is to transform the rough ashler into the perfect cube.

Seven and 12 form the two most important numerical patterns in the heavens. It is through the circle of the 12 signs of the Zodiac that the Celestial Hierarchies work in directing the evolution of the earth and all the kingdoms of life developing on it.

Biblical seers, understanding the forces of 12, use it repeatedly when dealing with events and characters of high spiritual import. In the Old Testament, the 12 sons of Jacob, representative of the 12 signs of the Zodiac is the most conspicuous example of the use of this number. Their work dominates the entire Old Testament.

Other instances of the use of 12 in the Bible include the 12 loaves of shew bread that were placed on the table in the inner court of the Tabernacle and which represent the opportunities for soul growth presented by the 12 solar months of the year. The Temple that Ezekiel beheld in a vision like the New

Jerusalem described by John, the Revelator, has twelve entrances, or avenues of service. The Christ chose 12 to work with Him in the initial dissemination of the evangelism of the new Christed Age.

Every esotericist understands that Twelve Forces grouped in a circle around one form a Unity that vibrates to 13. Herein lies the secret of plenty, peace, and power for all mankind. In the formula of 13 is to be found the occult key to the Master's words "Where two or three are gathered together in my Name, there am I in the midst of them." Through the proper assemblage of the forces of 12 and 1, or 13, "All the forces of heaven and earth are given unto you" as the Christ declared.

The wise Pythagoras taught that 1 is both limited and unlimited. When added rightly to 12, and thereby making 13, it is unlimited − the miracle of the loaves and fishes becomes an actuality on every plane of manifestation. Much of the work of the Christ and His 12 disciples is concerned with the powers of the mystic formula of 12 and 1.

Goethe, a master mind, had the power to tune in with the exalted forces of 13. He does so when describing the experiences of a Traveller on a visit to a certain Monastery wherein resided 12 Brothers together with a 13, who was head of the Group. The Traveller undergoes many trials before he discovers the home of the Order he seeks. The Monastery which he ultimately finds is crowned with a black cross which is embellished with 7 red roses. This same symbol also forms the gate through which the Traveller must enter before he can stand in the presence of the 12 and the exalted 13th.

In the great Hall of Accomplishment there were 13 chairs and above each hung a shield, showing in symbol the deeds performed by the one who was worthy to occupy that seat. The 13th synthesizes the forces of the encircling 12. The 12 notes of the chromatic scale are focused on a 13th which sounds the basic harmony of the octave. The Traveller arrives at the

Monastery just as the 13th Brother is preparing to ascend to higher realms, having mastered all the lessons belonging to material existence. It is a case of having completed a cycle – a cycle of 12 – and entering upon a new cycle in the ever ascending spiral of being. This portion of the story parallels the event in the life of the Christ when observing the initiatory Rite of the Last Supper prior to taking His departure from the 12 and later making His ascension.

Mem is the 13th letter of the Hebrew alphabet and represents the great feminine or Mother mystery. The processes of this mystery are fourfold, and may be described as birth, death, sublimation, and transfiguguration. The Book of Revelation, that most profoundly mystical of all Bible books, is keyed to 13, and the completion of the fourfold process, or consummation of the magic power of 13 is depicted in the glorious vision of the Woman clothed with the sun:

> "And there appeared a great wonder in heaven; a woman clothed with the Sun, and the moon under her feet, and upon her head a crown of twelve stars." (Revelation 12:1)

The letter Mem is the most important of the three Mother letters and is ranked by the Kabbalists as second in power only to the straight line (1) of Absolute Unity. The form of the letter Mem is similar to the symbol for the sign Aquarius the urn from which the shepherd of the skies is pouring water on the earth bears 13 stars.

The repeated use of 13 in the seal of the United States of America is not by mere chance, but in obedience to cosmic law as required by the nation's destiny. Thirteen means either death through failure and degeneration, or the attainment in regeneration of a New Order of the Ages. There are no half way measures with 13; it demands all or nothing. Thus is America's high calling portrayed numerically, If she be true to it, she will, under 13 inaugurate fresh beginnings for all the race.

The number 13 digits 4 which enfolds the powers of the Tetragrammaton, the Yod-He-Vau-He of the Ancients. A knowledge of that magic Name gives an open sesame into all the wonders of the heavens above and the waters under the earth.

And when Abram heard that his brother was taken captive, he armed his trained servants, born in his own house, three hundred and eighteen, and pursued them unto Dan. (Genesis 14:14.) — These trained servants in the house of Abram, 318 in number, digit 12 and indicate the time and place of preparation for a complete union with 13. In Greek these numbers give the beginning of the words meaning Jesus and the cross.

Lamed, interpreted as a spur of pain, is the 12th of the Hebrew letters and is described as the hanging man. By a proper training of the 318 = 12 servants, or the 12 faculties within, the personal life is mastered, or crucified, and a new Christed man is born. The 12th sign is Pisces, which governs the house of tears and sorrow. He who does the will of the Father enters into harmony with His plan and comes to know the truth that sets man free. Under the powers of 13 he attains to the heights of an ascended consciousness.

Anna Kingsford says in The Perfect Way: "As the number of the lunar months, thirteen is the symbol of the woman and denotes the soul and her reflection of God — the solar number twelve being that of spirit." — "The two numbers in combination form the perfect year of that dual humanity which alone is made in the image and likeness of God — the true Christian year, wherein the two, the inner and the outer, spirit and matter — are as one." — "Thirteen then represents that full union of man with God wherein Christ becomes Christ."

The literal translation for the 12th power-force of the sacred series, the Hebrew letter Lamed, is an oxgoad. In the life of man it operates as the influence of pain, sorrow, disillusionment. Call

107

it by whatsoever name we will, it is that unalterable law of destiny which sooner or later in the course of the many life cycles of man, brings him to that place wherein he knows that he cannot safely depend upon any other power than the spirit within. When he comes to this realization, then he can say with the Christ: "The Father and I are one," and "He doeth the works." With this realization comes the ability to understand and to receive the mighty spiritual outpourings of the powers operating through the forces of 12. – This was the state of consciousness attained by the Immortal Twelve who were chosen by the supreme Master. Their lives had each been beset with trials and difficultes, and many were the renunciations which they were called upon to make. It was the oxgoad of pain and travail which refined them in spirit so that they might hear the tender tones of the Master's voice whispering in their storm-stressed hearts, "Come and follow me."

It was this inner understanding of the divine purpose of sorrow which caused the early Christians to so revere the cross which represented to them the path that leads from the outer to the within, from the personal to the impersonal, from the seen which is temporal to the unseen which is eternal.

The mystic chant of Lamed is as follows: "Before this have I declared myself to be The Teacher of Teachers, and mine instruction is like unto a goad." – The "Teacher of all Teachers" is sorrow, and so we note the heavy impress of its hand upon the lives of men and races throughout the world. Humanity in the large, however, has not come to recognize the divine compensation that sorrow brings; and so strife, rebellion, are its present results; rather than the glory of at-one-ment which a complete surrender gives.

Every ideal for future attainment set forth in the Biblical records that is presented in the numerical terms of 12, as for example, the Temple of Ezekiel, the works of the Twelve Tribes, and the Eternal City of Revelation, have as their foundation stone the tears and blood, the sorrow and sacrifice of the people to whom the ideal was given. It is only through the awakening engendered by the forces of 12 that the illumination of 13 may be found. In Revelation, that mystic cycle of spiritual law which is attuned to the forces of this number of transformation John sings "God shall wipe away all tears for the former things have passed away." Sorrow and the tears it brings forth, will be necessary no longer, for man shall have come into the full realization of the glorious freedom in spirit which only a complete surrender of all things personal can give.

Thirteen has been considered since ancient times as the number of ill luck and misfortune. This is because its true significance has been totally uncomprehended. Thirteen means death or transfiguration — death if man chooses to follow the old ways of material living; transfiguration, if he accepts the new. The New Jerusalem of Revelation describes this last named condition. For the early Christians the powers of 13, the 12 and the 1, were typified by the 12 disciples and St. Paul who combined and synthesized all the 12 attributes of spirit represented by this illumined company united and conjoined with or in 13.

The Tarot symbology of the 13 power-force is that of a skeleton armed with a scythe, representing the inevitableness of death in the present dispensation of mortal thought. But a rainbow rises on the horizon, an emblem of the new day dawning in the race consciousness, and described in the Revelation of John as the concealed (save to the few) forces of the number 13.

From the Book of Tokens by Paul Case, we quote these lines of meditation as descriptive of this great force resident in the 13th letter Mem: "Absolve thyself in this Great Sea of the Waters of Life. Dive deep in it until thou hast lost thyself. And having lost thyself, thou shalt find thyself again, and be one with Me. Then shall the glory of Myself, which is thy true self, be mirrored in thee."

KEY THOUGHTS

"Twelve is 4 plus 8, or the world and man renewed. It is 4 x 3 or the world and man in intimate union with God, and it is 6 x 2, symbolic of Christ taking upon Himself the sins of man and becoming subject to death for the sake of man's redemption."